1001 Very Funny Jokes

Sandy Ransford has been hooked on humour ever since her first job in publishing – editing the jokes for a well-known magazine – and she has now written more joke books than she can count. Born in South Yorkshire (which may account for it), she now lives in rural mid-Wales surrounded by sheep, with her husband, a horse, a cat, two pygmy goats and two miniature ponies – all of which keep her laughing.

Jane Eccles is the ustrator of this hilarious collection of jokes. She ustrates from a sunny room in her lovely West London home, hardly bothered by the japeful interruptions of her young son and his collection of sharks. Her ustrations are filled with lightness and fun, for she always ustrates with a smile on her face.

Hard then to believe what happens when the weather turns colder and the first box of tissues appears on her desk to catch the sudden sneeze and unwelcome cough.

Jane Eccles turns into an ill-ustrator.

1001 Very Funny Jokes

Sandy Ransford

Illustrated by **Jane Eccles**

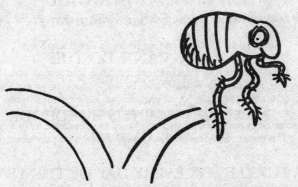

MACMILLAN CHILDREN'S BOOKS

First published 2004
by Macmillan Children's Books
a division of Macmillan Publishers Limited
20 New Wharf Road London N1 9RR
Basingstoke and Oxford
www.panmacmillan.com

Associated companies throughout the world

ISBN 0 330 42035 6

This collection copyright © Sandy Ransford 2004
Illustrations copyright © Jane Eccles 2004

The right of Sandy Ransford and Jane Eccles to be identified as the author and
illustrator of this book has been asserted by them in accordance with the
Copyright, Designs and Patents Act 1988.

3 5 7 9 8 6 4

A CIP catalogue record for this book is available from the British Library.

Printed by Mackays of Chatham plc, Chatham, Kent.

Contents

Animal Antics

What's the definition of a cat?
An animal that never cries over spilt milk.

Why did the cat join the Red Cross?
It wanted to be a first-aid kit.

What do cats eat for breakfast?
Mice Krispies.

What do cats read at breakfast?
Mewspapers.

What do you call a cat that's
eaten a duck?
A duck-filled fatty puss.

Why did the cat eat cheese?
So he could sit by a mousehole with baited breath.

What did the dog say when he sat on the sandpaper?
'Rough!'

'I've lost my dog. What shall I
  do?'
  'Why not put an advert in
  the local paper?'
    'Don't be silly, my dog
    can't read.'

ANDY: We've got a new dog. Would you like to come and see him?

MANDY: Does he bite?

ANDY: I don't know. That's why I want you to come round, you can help me to find out.

KERRY: Does your dog see off strangers?

TERRY: Only when he doesn't know them.

Did you hear about the dog who was so lazy that when his owner was watering the garden he never lifted a leg to help him?

A man took his dog into a restaurant, and sat him down in a chair at his table.

The waitress came up to him. 'I'm sorry, sir,' she said, 'but I'm afraid we don't allow dogs in this restaurant. You must take him outside.'

'But this dog is a very special dog,' said the man. 'He can talk.'

'I don't care if he can play the violin, he's not allowed in here,' said the waitress and, as the man refused to move the dog, she went to fetch the manager.

'I must ask you to take that dog out of the restaurant,' said the manager.

'But this dog can talk,' persisted the man.

'OK,' said the manager, 'if he can talk, get him to tell me what's above this restaurant.'

So the man asked the dog, who replied, 'R-r-r-oof.'

'There!' said the manager. 'I knew he couldn't talk. Out, both of you!'

When they were standing out on the pavement, the dog looked up and said to his master, 'Oh look, above the restaurant there's a hairdresser's.'

A man went to buy a horse he'd seen advertised in the paper. It was a very good-looking animal, with excellent paces, and it seemed friendly and easy to handle. The price being asked, however, was very cheap and, while this seemed like good news, it made the purchaser suspicious. So he asked the woman who was selling the horse if there was anything wrong with it.

'It's a very good horse,' she said, 'but it does have one small problem.'

'What's that?' asked the man.

'Well,' she replied, 'if it sees a pomegranate, it sits down on it.'

'A pomegranate?' said the man. 'You don't see many pomegranates where I live. I think I'll buy the horse.'

So he bought the horse, and set off to ride it home. They went up hill and down dale, and the horse behaved perfectly. The man felt very pleased with himself for managing to buy such a splendid animal so cheaply. Their way led through a small wood, through which flowed a stream they had to cross. The horse walked into the stream without any fuss, but when it got to the very middle, it stopped and sat down. The man urged it on, but it wouldn't budge.

'Hmm,' he thought, 'there must be a pomegranate in this stream.' So he got off the horse and waded about, but he could see no sign of any kind of fruit, let alone a pomegranate. He pulled on the horse's reins, shouted at it, and even thumped it on the rump, but it wouldn't move a muscle. Finally, in a very bad temper, the man abandoned the horse, and set off, dripping wet, to walk back to the place he had bought it from.

He walked into the stable yard where the woman who had sold him the horse was working, and told her what had happened. 'And,' he finished, 'I'll swear there wasn't a pomegranate anywhere near that stream!'

'Oh dear,' she replied. 'I quite forgot to tell you. He sits on fish too.'

What happens when a horse loses its shoes?
It has to run around in its socks.

FATHER: I'd like to hire a horse, please.
STABLE OWNER: Certainly, sir. How long?
FATHER: The longest you've got, I have four children.

How do you hire a horse?
Stand it on four bricks.

TRISHA: Is your pony well-mannered?
MISHA: Oh yes. Whenever we get to a fence he always stops and lets me go over first.

What did the horse say when he got to the end of his
nosebag?
'This is the last straw.'

How do you count cows?
With a cowculator.

What happens if you walk under a cow?
You might get a pat on the head.

A man's car broke down outside a farm and a cow
walked past, looked at it, and suggested he check the
petrol feed pipe. Amazed, the man staggered up to the
farmhouse and told the farmer.

'Was it a Friesian cow, a black and white one?' asked
the farmer.

'Yes,' replied the man.

'Then take no notice of her,' said the farmer.
'Friesians don't know a thing about cars.'

Did you hear about the cow who was so cold one
winter she didn't give milk, she gave ice cream?

An Englishman, an Irishman and a Scotsman were walking through a field when they met a cow. 'That's an English cow,' said the Englishman.

'No,' said the Irishman, 'it's an Irish cow.'

'You're both wrong,' said the Scotsman. 'It's a Scottish cow – look, it's got bagpipes underneath.'

FARMER: I can't decide whether to buy myself a bicycle or a new cow for the farm.
FRIEND: You'd look silly riding a cow.
FARMER: I'd look even sillier trying to milk a bicycle.

What did one pig say to the other?
'Let's be pen-friends.'

STACEY: I've just bought a pig.
TRACEY: Where are you going to keep it?
STACEY: In the kitchen.
TRACEY: But what about the smell and the mess?
STACEY: The pig will just have to get used to it.

What do you call high-rise flats for pigs?
Styscrapers.

FIRST SHEEP: Baa.
SECOND SHEEP: Moo.
FIRST SHEEP: What do you mean, moo?
SECOND SHEEP: I'm learning a foreign language.

KEVIN: Did you know it takes three sheep to make one jumper?
KYLIE: I didn't even know sheep could knit!

Where do sheep like to shop?
Woolworths.

What did the polite ram say as he waited to let his lady friend go through the gate first?
'After ewe.'

TEACHER: What makes you think fleas are white?
LAUREN: The nursery rhyme.
TEACHER: Which nursery rhyme?
LAUREN: You know, 'Mary had a little lamb, its fleas were white as snow.'

CHLOE: Where do fleas go in the winter?
ZOE: Search me!

What do you call a cheerful flea?
A hoptimist.

How do fleas travel around?
By itch-hiking.

What time is it when a fly and a flea pass each other?
Fly past flea.

How can you keep flies out of the kitchen?
Put a bucket of manure in the dining room.

What did the bee say to the bluebottle?
'I must fly now, but I'll give you a buzz later.'

When does a bee fly with its legs crossed?
When it's looking for a BP station.

Why do bees have sticky hair?
They use honey combs.

What's even more amazing than a talking dog?
A spelling bee.

Where do frogs sit?
On toadstools.

How do frogs make beer?
Well, they start with some hops.

What do you call a frog spy?
A croak and dagger agent.

Why do giraffes have such long necks?
To join their heads to their bodies.

Why do giraffes enjoy having such long necks?
Because their feet smell awful.

Why do giraffes eat breakfast very early?
So the food will be in their stomachs by lunchtime.

What is a zebra?
A horse behind bars.

What is a leopard?
A dotted lion.

A lion was prowling across the African plains one day when it met a wildebeest. 'Wildebeest,' said the lion, 'who is king of the jungle?'

'You are, of course,' replied the wildebeest.

The lion went on his way until he met a zebra. 'Zebra,' he said, 'who is king of the jungle?'

'You are, of course,' answered the zebra.

The lion continued his journey for a while, until he met a jackal. 'Jackal,' he asked, 'who is king of the jungle?'

'You are, of course,' replied the jackal.

On went the lion until he met an elephant. 'Elephant,' he asked, 'who is king of the jungle?'

The elephant looked at him for a moment. Then he reached forward, picked the lion up in his trunk, whirled him up in the air above his head, spun him round a few times and then hurled him into a nearby waterhole.

Wet, bruised and frightened, the lion struggled out of the water. 'OK, OK,' he said to the elephant, 'just because you don't know the answer there's no need to lose your temper.'

An explorer in Africa came face to face with a lion and was so frightened that he fainted. When he recovered, he saw that the lion seemed to be praying.

'Thank you for not eating me,' he said.

'Shh,' said the lion. 'I'm saying grace.'

Who went into the lion's den and came out alive?
The lion.

What's the difference between a thunderstorm and a lion with toothache?
One pours with rain, the other roars with pain.

When is a monkey like a flower?
When it's a chimp-pansy (chimpanzee).

How do monkeys make toast?
Put it under the g'rilla.

A gorilla went into a cafe and ordered a glass of orange juice, handing the proprietor a ten-pound note to pay for it. Thinking the ape would know nothing about money, the proprietor didn't give him any change.

'We don't often get gorillas in here,' he remarked.

'With orange juice at ten pounds a glass,' replied the gorilla, 'I'm not surprised.'

What did the gorilla say when he heard his sister had just had a baby gorilla?
'Well, I'll be a monkey's uncle!'

How can you tell when a gorilla's been in your fridge?
By the hairs in the butter.

What's the difference between a gorilla and a banana?
Have you ever tried peeling a gorilla?

What do you call an overweight gorilla?
A chunky monkey.

JENNY: Did you hear about the exhausted kangaroo?
BENNY: No, what about him?
JENNY: He was out of bounds.

BABY SKUNK: Please, Mum, can I have a chemistry set for Christmas?
MOTHER SKUNK: Certainly not. The house will smell terrible.

How many skunks does it take to make a terrible smell?
A phew.

How can you stop a skunk from smelling?
Put a clothes peg on its nose.

What's the difference between a skunk and a squirrel?
The skunk uses a cheaper deodorant.

What fur do you get from a skunk?
As fur as possible!

What kind of animal has wooden legs?
A timber wolf.

What do parrots eat?
Polyfilla.

Whose parrot sits on his shoulder squawking, 'Pieces of four! Pieces of four!'?
Short John Silver's.

A sailor was telling his friend about the time he was shipwrecked and almost died of starvation. 'It was awful,' he said. 'In the end I had to eat my pet parrot.'

'What did it taste like?' asked his friend.

'Chicken, duck, turkey – you name it, that bird could imitate anything!'

A woman bought two parrots in a cage. The shopkeeper warned her that one of the parrots was a bit aggressive, but she took them home anyway. The following morning, when she went to feed the parrots, she discovered that the aggressive one had killed the other. So she went out and bought a buzzard. 'This will teach it a lesson,' she thought.

Next morning, however, she discovered that the parrot had also killed the buzzard. Still determined to teach the destructive bird a lesson, she bought a huge eagle and put it in with the parrot.

The following day, when she uncovered the cage, there was the eagle, stone dead, and standing there, gloating, with not a feather left on its body, was the parrot. 'Phew!' it said to its owner, 'I really had to take my coat off to that one!'

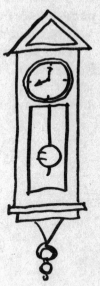

What goes cluck, cluck, bang!?
A chicken in a minefield.

On which side does a chicken have the most feathers?
The outside.

When is a turkey like an imp?
When it's a-gobblin'.

TEACHER: Can you name a bird that doesn't build its own nest?
NICKY: The cuckoo.
TEACHER: That's right. And how did you know that?
NICKY: Everybody knows that. Cuckoos live in clocks.

What happens to ducks before they grow up?
They grow down.

What happens to ducks when they fly upside down?
They quack up.

What kinds of birds might you see in church?
Birds of prey.

DEREK: Did you hear the story about the peacock?
ERIC: No.
DEREK: It's a beautiful tail.

Two pigeons were sitting chatting on a tree branch
wondering what to do next.

'You know that car showroom by the station?' asked
one.

'Yes,' said the other.

'Let's fly over there and put a deposit on a Rolls-
Royce.'

Crazy Crosses

What do you get if you cross a sheepdog with a jelly?
Colliewobbles.

What do you get if you
cross a sheepdog with a
bunch of daffodils?
Collieflowers.

What do you get if you cross
a dog with a vegetable?
A Jack Brussel.

What do you get if you cross a
dog with a ploughed field?
A mutt in a rut.

What do you get if you cross a dog with a
tractor?
A Land Rover.

What do you get if you
cross a gun dog with a
telephone?
A golden receiver.

What do you get if you
cross a cement mixer with a
chicken?
A bricklayer.

What do you get if you cross a
poodle with a chicken?
Pooched eggs.

What do you get if you cross a
woodpecker with a carrier
pigeon?
**A bird that knocks before it
delivers a message.**

What do you get if you cross a woodpecker with a
parrot?
A bird that talks to you in Morse code.

What do you get if you cross a pig with a zebra?
Striped sausages.

What do you get if you cross a pig with a billy goat?
A crashing boar.

What do you get if you cross a cow with
a camel?
Lumpy milkshakes.

What do you get if you cross a sheep
with a kangaroo?

**A woolly jumper with
pockets.**

What do you get if you cross a sheep with a
thunderstorm?
A wet blanket.

What do you get if you cross a lamb with a spaceship?
The star-sheep *Enterprise*.

What do you get if you cross a lamb with a penguin?
A sheepskin dinner jacket.

What do you get if you cross a giraffe with a dog?
An animal that barks at low-flying aircraft.

What do you get if you cross a hedgehog with a giraffe?
A very long hairbrush.

What do you get if you cross a duck with an earth
tremor?
An earthquack.

What do you get if you cross a cow with a duck?
Cream quackers.

What do you get if you cross a football team with an ice-cream cornet?
Aston Vanilla.

What do you get if you cross a chicken with an elephant?
A creature that remembers why it crossed the road.

What do you get if you cross a parrot with an elephant?
An animal that tells everything it remembers.

What do you get if you cross a parrot with a crocodile?
A creature that bites off your leg while saying, 'Who's a pretty boy, then?'

What do you get if you cross an owl with a skunk?
Something that smells but doesn't give a hoot.

What do you get if you cross a goose with a rubbish tip?
Down in the dumps.

What do you get if you cross an elephant with a bag of toffees?
Either toffees that never forget or an elephant that sticks your teeth together.

What do you get if you cross a cat with a ball of wool?
Mittens.

What do you get if you cross a locomotive with a packet of gum?
A chew-chew train.

What do you get if you cross a novel with a wheel?
A book that turns its own pages.

What do you get if you cross a rabbit with a flea?
Bugs Bunny.

What do you get if you cross a rabbit with a leek?
A bunion.

What do you get if you cross a fish with a pig?
Wet and dirty.

What do you get if you cross a hedgehog with an electrical fuse?
Barbed wire.

What do you get if you cross a space monster with a footballer?
I don't know, but when it takes a shot at goal no one tries to stop it!

What do you get if you cross a cat with a lemon?
A sourpuss.

What do you get if you cross an anthill with a greenhouse?
Ants in your plants.

What do you get if you cross a computer with a herb garden?
A thyme machine.

What do you get if you cross a computer with a policeman?
PC Plod.

What do you get if you cross a computer with Michael Schumacher?
A system that can crash at 200 miles per hour.

What do you get if you cross a dentist with a camera?
A man with a film on his teeth.

What do you get if you cross an athlete with a camera?
Film that develops itself at the gym.

What do you get if you cross a
scaredy-cat with a clock?
A nervous tick.

What do you get if you cross a TV
with a homing pigeon?
**A set that flies back to the shop if
you don't pay for it.**

Cracks from Cyberspace

What can access cyberspace but is very smelly?
A hum computer.

What do monkeys do
with computers?
**Send each other
chimpanz-eemail.**

What do athletes
do when they're
not running?
Surf the sprinternet.

What do fish do when they're
not swimming?
Surf the finternet.

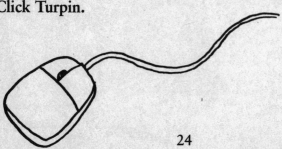

What grows on www.gardens.co.uk and stings?
Internettles.

Which famous highwayman was a computer nut?
Click Turpin.

How do sheep sign their emails?
Ewes sincerely.

Why did the idiot try to eat his computer?
Someone had told him it was an Apple.

What do you get if you cross a computer with a hamburger?
A Big Mac.

TEACHER: Now, children, you mustn't spend too much time on your computers, or you'll grow up to be very unfit and fat.
PUPIL: Gosh, sir, you must have spent an awful lot of time working on yours!

PUPIL: Should I turn on the computer with my right hand or my left hand?
TEACHER: Most people use the on/off switch.

DARREN: Have you seen the www.tomato.net website?
SHARON: No, but I'll try to ketchup with it next week.

GILL: Have you seen the fireworks website?
PHIL: Yes, it blew my mind.

How do vampires sign their emails?
Best vicious.

JENNY: Did you find www.fruitjellyandcream.com interesting?
PENNY: Not really, it was a trifle boring.

BOB: Have you seen the shipwreck website?
ROB: Yes, but it hasn't sunk in yet.

TILLY: Have you seen www.puttingupcurtains.com?
MILLY: Yes, but I can't seem to get the hang of it.

TIM: Have you seen that new website about trousers?
JIM: I don't like it, it's pants.

Gareth was buying a new computer, and the salesman displayed the latest model, saying enthusiastically, 'This computer is so quick it will cut your workload in half.'
   'Great!' said Gareth. 'I'll buy two of them.'

Why was the computer operator so bad-tempered?
Because he had a chip on his shoulder.

Why did the boy mouse like the girl mouse?
They just seemed to click.

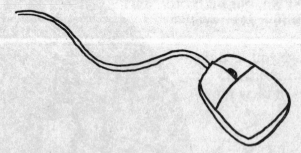

What happens to a computer mouse when it eats too quickly?
It gets click-ups.

Who can you chat to if you visit the Disney website?
Mick e-mouse.

How do winter sports enthusiasts communicate with each other?
By ski-mail.

How do insects communicate with each other?
By bee-mail.

How do fish communicate with each other?
By sea-mail.

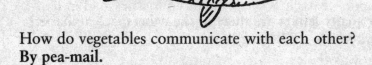

How do vegetables communicate with each other?
By pea-mail.

Why didn't the musical instruments email each other?
They preferred to write notes.

How can a flea learn to use a computer?
He has to start from scratch.

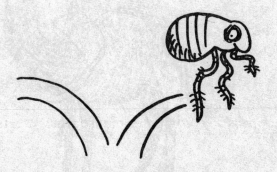

Why was the computer nut away from school?
He'd caught a computer bug.

What did Shakespeare say when he was sending a
message to his friend?
'To e or not to e, that is the question.'

What did the computer nut need an oil can?
His mouse was squeaking.

Why didn't the computer get on with the printer?
He wasn't her type.

How can you find a really cool website?
Put your computer in the fridge.

How many letters are there in the cyberspace alphabet?
Twenty-four – ET went home.

How did Vikings keep their emails secret?
They used Norse Code.

What makes people laugh on the internet?
Dot comics.

Why don't camels
surf the Net?
**It gives them
the hump.**

POLLY: Do you know the email address for the Morse Code website?
MOLLY: Yes, it's www.dash.dash.dash.com.

Did you hear about the world's first plane to be run entirely by computer? Mr Jones decided to try it out. The plane taxied slowly down the runway and stopped. Its door opened automatically. A flight of steps moved automatically up to the door, and a voice invited the passengers to board the plane. Mr Jones did so. When all the passengers were settled in their seats, a voice told them to fasten their seat belts.

The plane then began to move, preparatory to taking off. Another voice addressed the passengers: 'Good morning, ladies and gentleman. Welcome to the world's first fully automated plane. Everything this plane does is controlled by its computer. It works perfectly all the time. Absolutely nothing can go wrong, go wrong, go wrong, go wrong . . .'

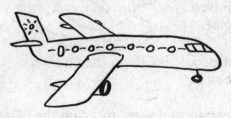

What's another name for software for Windows?
A polishing cloth.

What is a cursor?
Someone having problems with their computer.

What is computer hardware?
The part that makes a noise when you throw the machine through the window.

What do elves use computers for?
Doing their gnomework.

What do you call
www.squiggleswigglesandjaggededges.com?
A site for sore eyes.

When does your computer give
you a headache?
**When you bang your head
on it.**

What do keen surfers of
the Internet drink at
coffee breaks?
Netscafé.

What do builders
look for when
they surf the Net?
www.com.crete.

Why didn't the
butterflies look at
websites?
Their mother had told them to avoid the Net.

What did one spider say to his friend?
'Welcome to my website.'

What did the computer mouse say when it was learning
to dance?
'Slow, slow, click, click, slow.'

What can you order at the Internet cafe?
Tea-mail.

Did you know there are only two kinds of computer?
One is the latest model, the other is obsolete.

BONNIE: What do you think of www.wetpaint.com?
RONNIE: It's a bit tacky.

ANNIE: Does your mum shop on the Internet?
DANNY: No, she says the shopping trolley keeps falling off the computer.

What goes, 'Choo, choo, choo,' while surfing the Internet?
Thomas the Search Engine.

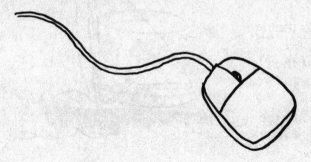

Why did the lumberjack get nowhere with the Internet?
He was always logging on and off.

Daft Definitions

You won't find these definitions in any dictionary, but they describe what some words *ought* to mean.

A

amazon – very surprising
annexe – it's Anne's turn next
aperitif – a set of dentures
arbour – where boats are tied up

asbestos – as good as the next person
assent – the smell of a donkey
aster – put a question to her
axe – what you do with a question

B

barometer – something that measures the contents of barrows
belong – keep someone waiting around
bison – what you wash your hands in

bizarre – a jumble sale
blubber – to whale
bruise – makes a pot of tea

C

cartoon – music played in a car
catkin – the pet puss's relatives
cattle – place to keep cats (as in kennel)
chimpanzee – a flower planted by a monkey
climate – what you do with a mountain
code – what you have when your nose runs

D

dandelion – large cat that's very fussy about his
    appearance

design – de notice that tells you what to do
diet – what a man from Wales eats
doughnut – desist from doing

E

each – what makes you scratch
earwig – false hair with a built-in hearing-aid
e.g. – what a h.e.n. lays
engineer – what an engine hears with
Eton – been put into the mouth, chewed and swallowed
eureka – rude way of telling someone that they smell
expire – a church spire that's fallen down
explain – to parachute from an aircraft

F

faith – the part of a person you look at when they are
   speaking to you
famous – well-known mouse, such as Mickey
fiddlesticks – pieces of wood used to play a violin
fjord – a make of car found in Norway

flattery – living in apartments
foibles – what Aesop wrote

G

gargoyle – what you do when you have a sore throat
gorilla – the part of a cooker that makes the toast
grammar – your mother's or father's mother

granary – where your mother's or father's mother lives

guest – didn't know the answer but had a stab at it

H

halo – what one angel says to another
 when they meet

harvest – the garment she wears
 under her shirt

hence – birds that lay lots of eggs

hermit – a girl's hand

humbug – an insect that knows the
 tune but not the words

I

icicle – what an Eskimo pedals

icons – nuts from which oak trees grow

igloo – an Eskimo's toilet

insecticide – suicide by an insect

intent – on a camping holiday

J

jeep – a vehicle that doesn't cost very much

Juno – have you any idea?

K

karate – an orange root vegetable

kernel – the nut in charge of a regiment

ketchup – get level with everyone else

khaki – what you open the car's
 door with

kidnap – the baby's asleep

kindred – dislike of your family

kipper – person who spends most of their time asleep

knowledge – shelf on which reference books are kept

Korea – how you earn your living

L

lapse – what a cat does with a bowl of milk

launch – midday meal on a boat

lobster – cricket player who is a bad bowler

M

maximum – overweight mother

mayor – female horse

melancholy – a sad sheepdog

millennium – insect with lots of legs

mince – sweets with holes in the middle

minimum – very small mother

monkey – key to the door of a monastery
moose – Scottish rodent
myth – unmarried female moth

N

Nicholas – not wearing underwear
nightingale – wild and stormy evening
noose – what we read in newspapers
nun – nothing

O

octopus – cat with eight legs
offal – really terrible
operetta – person who works for British Telecom

P

panther – person who makes trousers
parasite – person who comes from Paris
pas de deux – father of twins
peace – vegetables that come out of a pod
pitcher – what an artist produces

Q

quiche – affectionate gesture
quicksand – fast egg-timer

R

ramshackle – chain used to tie up a male sheep
retail – give an animal another tail
ringleader – the first person in the bath
robin – bird that steals
robot – boat propelled by oars
rocket – swing it gently to and fro
Russian – moving around very quickly

§

sample – that's enough
sari – an apology
selfish – what a fishmonger does
shampoo – imitation poo
soot – clothing worn by a chimney sweep
spider – saw her

T

tax – nails paid to the government
tease – cups of hot drinks
tock – language a clock uses
tortoise – what the teacher did
 transparent – see-through mum or dad

urchin – part of 'er face
Urdu – hairstyle

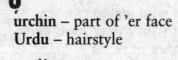

vanguard – person who
 protects a van
 village – will get older
 vixen – the vicar's son

W

wade – stay there a moment
wick – seven days
wind – past tense of 'win'
wombat – bat you play wom with
writer – person who makes things
 correct

X

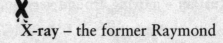

X-ray – the former Raymond

Y̌

yak – animal that talks a lot
yashmak – what Yash wears to keep her dry in the rain

Z̧

zinc – where we wash the dishes

What an Insult!

BERNIE: I didn't come here to be insulted!
ERNIE: Really? Where do you usually go?

GREG: I shouldn't lean out of the window like that.
GRANT: Why not?
GREG: Everyone will think it's Hallowe'en.

JULIA: You remind me of the sea.
JULIAN: Because I'm wild, untamed and romantic?
JULIA: No, because you make me feel sick.

ROMEO: How could I ever leave you?
ROWENA: By bus, car, train . . .

CAROL: It's time I left. Don't bother to show me to the door.
DARRYL: It's no bother, it will be a pleasure.

BILLY: Will you be my wife one day?
LILY: Not likely! I won't even be your wife for one hour!

HANNAH: I thought you were
going to marry Charlie. You said it
was love at first sight.
**ANNA: It was, but the second and third
sights put me off.**

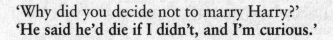

'Why did you decide not to marry Harry?'
'He said he'd die if I didn't, and I'm curious.'

There was once a man who was very lonely, so he tried
to make friends by joining an email friendship society.
He got in touch with several people, and he wrote lots
and lots of emails. He became very fond of one
particular lady, who wrote to him regularly, and
eventually he plucked up the courage to suggest they
meet.

He wrote in his message: 'I haven't mentioned this to
you before, but I'm not a very handsome man. I'm
seven feet tall, and I weigh twenty stone. I have a skin
complaint, so my face is covered in red patches. I have
scars on my cheeks from a bad attack of chickenpox. I
also have odd-coloured eyes – the right one is blue, the
left one is brown. I have one leg
shorter than the other, so I walk
with a limp. If after you've
read this you still want
to meet me, I'll be
outside the Cosy
Corner Cafe at 1 p.m.
on Wednesday.'

His lady friend
wrote back: 'Your
looks aren't important
to me, but our
friendship is. I look

forward very much to meeting you on Wednesday. Do you think you could carry a copy of *The Times* so I will recognize you?'

SINGER: Did you notice how my voice filled the whole theatre?
AGENT: Yes, and did you notice how many people left to make room for it?

GIRLFRIEND: There's something I'd like to give you.
BOYFRIEND: What's that?
GIRLFRIEND: A push through the door!

'He said he'd go to the ends of the earth for me.'
'And what did you say?'
'I told him when he got there he'd better jump off.'

'My brother's good at everything he does.'
'As far as I can see he usually does nothing!'

GAIL: My sister plays the violin. She's had many requests.'
GLORIA: So I've heard. But I gather she keeps on playing anyway.

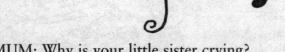

MUM: Why is your little sister crying?
JOHN: We were talking about fighting air pollution in school today.
MUM: Why did that make her cry?
JOHN: Because I said she could help fight it by stopping breathing.

'I wouldn't say he's stupid but he'd have trouble spelling "Anna" backwards.'

'Music has a terrible effect on Nigel.'
'What kind of effect?'
'It makes him play his bagpipes.'

'I see more of Jake than I used to do.'
'Yes, well, he's put on quite a lot of weight, hasn't he?'

DONNY: My business has failed, so I'm afraid I'm about to go bankrupt.
BONNIE: Oh, what a shame. I shall really miss you.

'Are they on speaking terms?'
'Put it this way, she's on speaking terms, he's on listening terms.'

'He thinks he's a big cheese.'
'That figures – I always have to hold my nose when I'm near him.'

'There's never a dull moment when Mike's around.'
'No, the dullness stretches endlessly for hours!'

MILLY: He said he'd go through anything for me.
TILLY: And has he?
MILLY: So far he's only gone through my bank account.

AMY: You remind me of a builder's bum.
JAMIE: How do you mean?
AMY: You're full of barefaced cheek!

'Why do you look so pale this morning?'
'I've just washed my face.'

'What's that peculiar smell?'
'Soap – I might have known you wouldn't recognize it!'

'Why are you washing your hands in black water?'
'Er, it wasn't black when I started.'

'Do you think the boys in the school football team smell?'
'Yes, people say they don't so much run up and down the field, as aroma round.'

What did Mrs Hardheart throw her husband when he was drowning in the river?
A goodbye kiss.

LENNY: If we got married, do you think you'd be able to live on my income?
JENNY: Oh yes. But what would you live on?

MRS SMITH, AT DOOR: Yes, can I help you?
SALESMAN: Good afternoon, madam. Can I sell you any cleaning materials?
MRS SMITH: No, thank you.
SALESMAN: No dusters, cloths or polishes?
MRS SMITH: No, thank you.
SALESMAN: No detergents, mops, brushes?
MRS SMITH: No, thank you.
SALESMAN: Don't you want any cleaning things at all?
MRS SMITH: No.
SALESMAN: I thought as much. Your neighbour said you never used any!

CARRIE: Did you hear that Mike was at medical school?
LARRY: No, I didn't know he was studying to be a doctor.
CARRIE: He's not, they're studying him!

MRS PLUMP: I think I've put on a bit of weight.
MRS PLIMP: Pull up a couple of chairs and tell me all about it.

JIM: Dave thinks he's a really hard man.
TIM: He will be when we've poured this concrete over him.

MIKE: Mervyn reckons he's a big noise round here.
SPIKE: He should eat fewer cans of beans then.

'Can I come fishing with you?'
'No, I've got enough maggots already.'

'I'm going to thump that Damon, he said I was stupid.'
'Don't take any notice of him, he's only repeating what everybody else says.'

'I don't know what Adam will do when he grows up, the poor lad is so ugly.'
'He could cure people of their hiccups.'

ADRIAN: I only sing when I'm in the bath.
ALISON, sniffing: I guess you don't sing that often!

GRAHAM: What were you before you met me?
GLORIA: Happy!

CAROL: What kind of man would you like to marry?
CHRISTINE: One who is clever enough to make lots of money, and stupid enough to spend it all on me.

HOSTESS: Did you like my chocolate cake?
VISITOR: Yes, did you buy it yourself?

'They say his father was an optician.'
'Is that why he's always making such a spectacle of himself?'

MR JONES: Is your wife very dear to you?
MR MOANS: I'll say! She costs me a fortune!

FIRST PLAYER: I love football. I could play like this for ever.
SECOND PLAYER: Don't you ever want to improve?

FIRST PLAYER: How would you have played that last shot?
SECOND PLAYER: In disguise!

TEACHER: Complete this proverb: 'A friend in need . . .'
TRISHA: Is a nuisance!

'I hear Dan has a leaning towards redheads.'
'Yes, but they keep pushing him back.'

'They say he was cut out to be a great success.'
'The trouble is, no one put the pieces together properly.'

'Why did you say your girlfriend reminds you of a Greek statue? Is it because she's very beautiful?'
'Yes, she's beautiful, but it's really because she's not all there.'

'Why do you call your brother Fog?'
'Because he's thick and wet.'

'Why do they call your sister Peach?'
'Because she's got a heart of stone.'

FREDDIE: Thank you so much for lending me that money. I shall be always in your debt.
TEDDY: That's what I'm worried about!

CLAIRE: I have a really soft spot for you.
CLIVE: Really?
CLAIRE: Yes, in the middle of a muddy pond.

SALLY: I wish you were a headache.
WALLY: Why?
SALLY: Because if you were I could take an aspirin and you'd go away.

PETER: What's the difference between your face and a rosebud?
ANITA: I don't know.
PETER: A rosebud is beautiful.

MAGGIE: You remind me of my nose.
AGGIE: What do you mean?
MAGGIE: You smell!

'Do you like me being around?'
'Yes, as long as you're not around too often.'

BILLY: How do you spell 'idiot' with just one letter?
MILLY: I don't know.
BILLY: U.

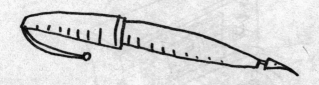

LEO: Do you know, you'd make a perfect . . .
THEO: What?
LEO: Stranger!

MRS BLACK: I am hoping to be given diamonds for
our wedding anniversary.
**MRS WHITE: Knowing
your Jim I reckon it's more
likely to be spades or clubs!**

VIOLINIST: I play chamber music.
NON-FAN: Hmm, sounds more like torture-chamber music.

'Do you think I should grow my hair long?'
'Yes, long enough to cover your face.'

'They say she's highly strung.'
'I knew she reminds me of a badly tuned piano.'

HORACE: Veronica had such a pretty chin when she was a girl . . .
MAURICE: She obviously thinks you can't have too much of a good thing, she's added a couple more now.

DANNY: I said, have you ever been out with someone uglier than me?
ANNIE: I know, I heard you the first time. I'm still thinking about the answer.

MRS DIM: My husband buys me a book on my birthday every year.
MRS GRIM: Really? You must have a very large library!

'Why do you say he's like a summer cold?'
'Because he's almost impossible to get rid of!'

'He has a Roman nose.'
'Yes, it looks as if it's roamin' here, roamin' there . . .'

Giant Laughs

What's a jumbo jet?
A flying elephant.

Where would you weigh a whale?
At a whale-weigh station.

What do you call a baby whale that cries a lot?
A little blubber.

What would you do with a charging rhinoceros?
Take away his credit card.

What weighs two tonnes and wears flowers in its hair?
A hippie-potamus.

What did the river say when the hippo sat down in it?
'Well, dam me!'

How can you get an elephant into a matchbox?
By taking out the matches first.

What time is it when an elephant sits on your sofa?
Time to buy a new sofa.

How can you tell when an elephant's been raiding your fridge?
By the footprints in the butter.

What happens when an elephant hides under your bed?
Your head hits the ceiling.

Why couldn't the elephant travel on a train?
Because his trunk wouldn't fit on the luggage rack.

When two elephants went to the seaside, why could only one of them go swimming?
They only had one pair of trunks.

Where can you buy a very ancient elephant?
At a mammoth sale.

How does an elephant climb an oak tree?
Sits on an acorn and waits until it grows.

How does an elephant get down from an oak tree?
Sits on a leaf and waits until autumn.

A policeman was walking slowly round his beat when he turned a corner and saw a man carefully spreading white powder all over the street. He watched him for a moment or two, and then walked up to him, gave a little cough, and said, 'Excuse me, sir, but what are you doing?'

The man looked up. 'Oh, morning, officer,' he said cheerily. 'I'm spreading elephant powder.'

'What,' asked the policeman, 'is elephant powder?'

'It's powder to keep elephants away,' replied the man.

'But there aren't any elephants round here,' said the policeman, more puzzled than ever.

'I know,' said the man happily. 'It just shows how well it works, doesn't it?'

What do you give an over-excited elephant?
Trunkquillizers.

What do you call an elephant with a television on its stomach?
An eletubby.

What is very large, green and has a trunk?
An unripe elephant.

What would you do with a blue elephant?
Try to cheer it up.

What's the difference between an African elephant and an Indian elephant?
About 5,000 kilometres.

What's the best way to raise an elephant?
With a forklift truck.

Why did the elephant paint his toenails red?
So he could hide in a strawberry patch.

Have you ever seen an elephant in a strawberry patch?
No.
Well, it shows how good the disguise is, doesn't it?

What's red on the outside, grey on the inside and very crowded?
A bus full of elephants.

Why did the elephants leave the circus?
They were tired of working for peanuts.

What do you call email from an elephant?
E-normous.

How do you tell a monster from an elephant?
A monster can't remember anything.

How does a monster count up to thirty-five?
On its fingers!

What does a monster do when he loses a hand?
Visits a second-hand shop.

Why did the monster go to see a psychiatrist?
Because he thought everyone loved him.

MUMMY MONSTER:
Why don't you go
outside and play with
your brother?
LITTLE MONSTER:
Because I'm tired of kicking
him around.

Why was the monster a
hopeless dancer?
Because he had three left feet.

Where did the lady
monster have her hair
done?
At the ugly parlour.

How do you greet a three-headed monster?
'Hello, hello, hello.'

Why does a monster forget everything you tell it?
Because it goes in one ear and out of all the others.

What's the best way to talk to a monster?
On the telephone.

What do you call a good-looking, gentle and polite
monster?
A failure.

What do you do if a monster sneezes?
Stand well back!

What kind of monster has the best hearing?
The eeriest.

What did the monster
say to the piano?
**'What beautiful teeth
you've got.'**

What's large, ugly, red-
faced and hides in a
corner?
**An embarrassed
monster.**

Where does a two-tonne
monster sit when it goes
to the cinema?
Anywhere it likes!

What happens if a two-tonne monster sits in front of
you at the cinema?
You miss most of the film.

Do monsters go on safaris?
Not safaris I know!

What's the difference between a monster
and a biscuit?
You can't dip a monster in your tea.

Where do you find monster snails?
**On the ends of monsters'
fingers.**

What should you do if a
monster breaks down your
front door?
Run out of the back door.

BOY MONSTER: Did you roll your eyes at me?
GIRL MONSTER: Yes.
BOY MONSTER: Would you like me to roll them back again?

Is it hard to bury a dead monster?
Yes, it's a huge undertaking.

What would you do if you found a monster with a broken toe?
Ring for a tow truck.

'What's the difference between a monster and a tomato?'
'I don't know.'
'Have you ever tried putting a monster in your salad?'

What goes flap, flap, flap, flap, flap, squelch?
A monster with one wet trainer.

What's the difference between a flea and a monster?
A monster can have fleas but a flea can't have monsters!

Why did the monster wear sunglasses?
So no one would recognize him.

On the Shelf

Have you ever read any of these books?

Light and Heat *by Alec Tricity*
Parachute Jumping *by Hugo Furst*
Catalogue Shopping *by May Lauder*
Looking into the Future *by Claire Voyant*
Waiting Patiently *by Arfur Minute*
Time Off *by Holly Day*
Telling Fibs *by Eliza Lott*
Enjoying Music *by Alison Tomyradio*
Russian Novels *by Warren Peace*
Snack Lunches *by Roland Hamm*
Going Home Early *by Tamara Isanotherday*
Broad River *by Bridget Over*
Flash Flood *by Marcella Sfullowater*
French Fries *by Crispin Themiddle*
Playing Whist *by Delia Cardsout*
Help! I'm Drowning! *by Dwayne Debathtub*
Can You Hear It? *by Isabel Ringing*

Policing the City *by Lauren Order*

Man Overboard! *by Mandy Lifeboats*

Going Shopping *by Tobias Somefood*

Selling Carpets *by Walter Wall*

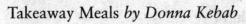

Studying Buildings *by R. K. Tecture*

Takeaway Meals *by Donna Kebab*

Chemistry Experiments *by Tess Tube*

In the Chemistry Lab *by A. Sid Test*

A Knock on the Head *by Esau Starrs*

Delicious Food *by Philippa Plate*

English Breakfasts *by Chris P. Bacon*

Playing Music *by Vi O'Linn*

Percussion Band *by Tam Borreen and Beata Drum*

Road Transport *by Laurie Driver*

Old Cars *by Maurice Minor*

Late for Work *by Miss D. Buss*

Padded Seating *by Ivor Bigbum*

Happy Birthday! *by Bess Twishes*

Modern Hairstyles *by Shaun Allover*

Polar Exploration *by Anne Tarctic*

Marathon Running *by Willy Makeit and Betty Wont*

Creepy Tales *by Denise R. Knocking*

Vegetarian Breakfasts *by Egbert Nobacon*

Quick Snacks *by Egon Toast*

Working the Night Shift *by Daisy Sleeps*

Running a Ferry *by Iona Boat*

Blushing Easily *by Timmy Denshy*

Puppet Shows *by Marion Ette*

Ringing the Bell *by Ken I. Comein*

Insect Bites *by Amos Quito*

Risking Arrest *by Kermit Acrime*

Living in Norway *by I. C. Winters*

Happy Holidays *by Sonny Skies*

What's Up, Doc?

'Doctor, doctor, can you help me out?'
'Certainly, which way did you come in?'

'Doctor, doctor, I keep thinking I'm a goat.'
'How long has this been going on?'
'Ever since I was a kid!'

'Doctor, doctor, I keep thinking I'm a racehorse!'
'Take these pills every four furlongs.'

'Doctor, doctor, my brother thinks he's a chicken.'
'We'd better send him to hospital.'
'No, you can't do that!'
'Why not?'
'We need the eggs.'

PATIENT: I think I have a dual personality.
PSYCHIATRIST: Then one of you had better wait
outside, this consultation is completely confidential.

HOSPITAL SISTER: This patient doesn't seem to be getting on very well with the new drip.
NURSE: No, I think he got on better with the doctor he used to have.

'Doctor, doctor, I feel like a pair of curtains.'
'Pull yourself together, man.'

'Doctor, doctor, I think I'm a dog.'
'Sit down, please.'
'I can't, I'm not allowed on the furniture.'

'Doctor, doctor, I keep stealing things. Can you help me?'
'Take these pills, and if they don't work, bring me a CD player.'

'Doctor, doctor, do I need glasses?'
'You certainly do, this is a greengrocer's.'

'Doctor, doctor, I keep seeing double.'
'Just sit down on the chair, please.'
'Which one?'

DOCTOR: I think the pains in your right leg are caused by old age.
OLD MAN: But my left leg is just as old and that doesn't hurt!

'Doctor, doctor, what are you writing on my toes?'
'A footnote.'

'Doctor, doctor, my sister thinks she's a lift.'
'Bring her in to see me.'
'I can't, she doesn't stop at this floor.'

'Doctor, doctor, I feel like a needle.'
'Yes, I can see your point.'

What did one doctor say when he met the other doctor?
'You look well, how am I?'

'Doctor, doctor, I think there's something wrong with my stomach.'
'Keep your coat on and no one will notice.'

'Doctor, doctor, can you give me something for wind?'
'Certainly, here's a kite.'

'Doctor, doctor, every bone in my body aches.'
'Be thankful you're not a herring.'

'Doctor, doctor, I'm at death's door.'
'Don't worry, I'll soon pull you through.'

'Doctor, doctor, can you cure my measles?'
'I never make rash promises.'

'Doctor, doctor, I feel like a yo-yo.'
'Sit down, sit down, sit down.'

'Doctor, doctor, I seem to be invisible.'
'Who said that?'

'Doctor, doctor, I think I'm a thief!'
'Have you taken anything for it?'

'Doctor, doctor, I feel like a billiard ball.'
'Go to the back of the queue.'

'Doctor, doctor, if I take this medicine will I get better?'
'Well, no one I've given it to has ever come back.'

'Doctor, doctor, I feel like an old sock.'
'Well, I'll be darned.'

'Doctor, doctor, people think I'm a cricket bat.'
'How's that?'
'Oh, not you as well!'

'Doctor, doctor, I feel like a bird.'
'Perch over there and I'll tweet you in a moment.'

'Doctor, doctor, I think I'm a computer.'
'Hmm, yes, you look as if you've got a virus.'

'Doctor, doctor, I feel like a pack of cards.'
'Sit down and I'll deal with you later.'

'Take one of these pills three times a day.'
'How can I take it more than once?'

'Doctor, doctor, I'm worried about my figure.'
'You'll have to diet.'
'What colour?'

'Doctor, doctor, I'm having trouble with my breathing.'
'I'll soon put a stop to that.'

'Doctor, doctor, my baby's swallowed my pen. What shall I do?'
'Use a pencil until I get there.'

'Doctor, doctor, my hair's falling out. Can you give me something to keep it in?'
'Certainly, here's a plastic bag.'

'Doctor, doctor, I've swallowed a spoon. What shall I do?'
'Lie down and don't stir.'

'Doctor, doctor, how can you cure water on the brain?'
'With a tap on the head.'

'Doctor, doctor, my friends think I'm mad because I like hard-boiled eggs.'
'What's wrong with that? I like hard-boiled eggs too.'
'Really? Would you like to come round and see my collection, I've got hundreds!'

'Doctor, doctor, I think I'm a bridge!'
'Whatever's come over you?'

'Doctor, doctor, I feel like a bell.'
'Give me a ring sometime.'

'Doctor, doctor, I've
swallowed a mouth organ.
What shall I do?'
'Be grateful you don't play
the piano.'

'Doctor, doctor, I feel
like a window.'
'Do you have a pane?'

'Doctor, doctor, I feel
like a wasp.'
'Just buzz off, will you!'

'Doctor, doctor, I feel like a dog.'
'Yes, I can see you're barking.'

'Doctor, doctor, I keep shrinking.'
'You'll just have to be a little patient.'

'Doctor, doctor, how long do I have to live?'
'Well, if I were you I wouldn't start following any
serials.'

'Doctor, doctor, I've
swallowed a roll of
film.'
'Let's hope nothing
develops.'

'Doctor, doctor, my uncle says he's got one foot in the grate.'
'You mean the grave?'
'No, the grate, he wants to be cremated.'

An old man who was terribly fussy about his health lived next door to a doctor, whose life he made a complete misery. He regularly visited the doctor's surgery, but, not content with that, would knock on his door late at night, and ask, 'Doctor, can you give me something for stomach ache,' or, 'Doctor can you give me something for a sore throat,' or, 'Doctor, can you give me something for a headache?'

The poor doctor got very fed up with all this, and was considering moving house when, to his great relief, the man died. He was buried in the local graveyard, and the doctor looked forward to a more peaceful life.

However, a few days later the doctor was knocked down by a bus, and also died. He was buried in the local graveyard, by a strange quirk of fate, right next to the grave of his former neighbour. That night, the doctor heard a tapping on the side of his coffin, and a familiar voice said, 'Doctor, can you give me something for worms?'

'Doctor, doctor, I keep feeling as if I'm boiling!'
'Just simmer down, will you?'

'Doctor, doctor, I feel so run down.'
'I'd advise you to be more careful when crossing the road.'

'Doctor, doctor, I've just swallowed two brown, three red and one pink snooker balls. What should I do?'
'Eat some greens and you'll soon be all right.'

'Doctor, doctor, I can't remember anything.'
'How did you get on with those pills I prescribed you?'
'What pills?'

'Doctor, doctor, I keep thinking I'm a gooseberry.'
'You are in a jam, aren't you?'

'Doctor, doctor, I've got a splinter in my finger.'
'Did you scratch your head?'

'Doctor, doctor, I can't get into my house! Will you help me, please?'
'Certainly, but what's it got to do with me?'
'The baby's swallowed the front-door key.'

'Doctor, doctor, I feel just like my old self again.'
'That means you need more treatment.'

'Doctor, doctor, how can I stop my nose running?'
'Stick out your foot and trip it up.'

'Doctor, doctor, I swallowed a clock last year.'
'Why didn't you come to see me sooner?'
'I didn't want to alarm anybody.'

'Doctor, doctor, do you know what's wrong with me?'
'I'm not sure, but it might be the drink.'
'OK, I'll come back when you're sober.'

'Doctor, doctor, I think I'm a slice of bread.'
'Stop loafing around.'

'Doctor, doctor, I think I've been bitten by a vampire.'
'Drink this water.'
'Will it make me feel better?'
'No, but I'll be able to see if your neck leaks.'

Kicking the Bucket

Down the road his funeral goes
As sobs and sighs diminish.
He died from drinking varnish –
He had a lovely finish.

Beneath this stone, a lump of clay
Lies Uncle Peter Dan'els,
Who early in the month of May
Took off his winter flannels.

Here lies a man who met his fate
Because he put on too much weight.
To overeating he was prone –
Now he's gained his final stone.

His death, it brought us bitter woe,
And to the heart it wrung us.
And all because he didn't know
A mushroom from a fungus.

HOSPITAL VISITOR: Are you all right? You look a little pale.
HOSPITAL PATIENT: That's because I nearly kicked the bucket.

Where do all good turkeys go when they die?
To oven.

What was the last thing King Charles I did?
Took his pet spaniel for a walk round the block.

What's the definition of a guillotine?
A pain in the neck.

INSURANCE SALESMAN: You need one of our Extra Special policies.
HOUSEHOLDER: What are they?
INSURANCE SALESMAN: They cover all eventualities. While you're in this world, they insure your life. Once you're in the next, they insure you against fire.

Young Jimmy didn't get on very well with his father, who was always finding fault with him.

'Why don't you try the old soft-soap treatment?' suggested his friend Jack.

'I did,' answered Jimmy. 'But he spotted it at the top of the stairs.'

An Apache chief called Shortcake lived with his squaw in a tepee on a reservation. One day Shortcake died, and a friend asked his squaw what she was going to do with him. She replied sadly, 'Squaw bury Shortcake.'

What's the difference between an Englishman frozen to death and a Scotsman at the South Pole?
One is killed with the cold, the other is cold with the kilt.

What do you call an ancient Egyptian who eats biscuits in bed?
A crumby mummy.

What's the difference between a musician and a corpse?
One composes, the other decomposes.

What kind of riddle do travellers who climb to the top of a pyramid find?
A cone under 'em.

FIRST MAN: I hear Mr Twiddle has died. Did he leave his wife much?
SECOND MAN: **Oh yes, almost every week.**

FIRST MAN: Why do you say you want to be buried at sea?
SECOND MAN: **Because my wife says she wants to dance on my grave.**

ALI: Why do you say bungee jumping is a deadly poison?
SALLY: One drop and you're dead.

MAN ON PHONE: A box for four, please.
ANSWERING VOICE ON PHONE: I'm sorry, we don't have boxes for four, just boxes for one.
MAN ON PHONE: Is that the Lyceum Theatre?
ANSWERING VOICE: No, it's Jones's the undertakers.

What's the last thing you do before you die?
You bite the dust.

How does someone become a coroner?
Well, first they have to pass some stiff exams.

CLIENT: I want you to bury my wife.
UNDERTAKER: But I buried your wife last year.
CLIENT: That was my first wife. I remarried.
UNDERTAKER: Oh, congratulations.

How do undertakers speak?
Gravely.

How do undertakers fasten their ties?
With wreath knots.

What's an undertaker's least favourite saying?
'Never say die.'

In which town do undertakers really feel at home?
Gravesend.

'Did you hear they are going to build a wall round the cemetery?'
'No, why's that?'
'Because so many people are dying to get in.'

FIRST GARDENER: I used to work with hundreds under me, you know.
SECOND GARDENER: Really? When was that?
FIRST GARDENER: When I used to cut the grass at the cemetery.

FIRST MAN, ON PHONE: Did you see the announcement of my death in the local paper?
SECOND MAN: Yes. Where are you calling from?

Gran always read the death notices in the local paper, so she could keep track of the people she knew who had died. One day when she was scanning down the columns, she looked up with a puzzled expression on her face.
'What's the matter?' asked Grandad.
'Every time I read the obituary column, it surprises me,' she replied.
'Why do people always die in alphabetical order?'

A wealthy old man was getting very frail, and his doctor, who had looked after him for many years and knew him very well, suggested that perhaps it was time he made his will.

'I've already done that,' said the patient. 'I'm leaving all my money to the doctor who saves my life.'

PATIENT'S WIFE: Why did you say you had both good news and bad news?
NURSE: Well, the bad news is that your husband died this morning. The good news is that the man in the next bed wants to buy his dressing-gown and slippers.

PATIENT: Doctor, doctor, I think I'm dying.
DOCTOR: Dying? That's the last thing you will do!

WIFE, AT SICK HUSBAND'S BEDSIDE: Is there no hope, doctor?
DOCTOR: That depends on what you're hoping for.

A funeral procession made its way slowly along the road, and a passer-by asked a little boy who was watching who it was that had died. 'The man in the coffin,' replied the lad.

BEN: Why did Annie get the sack from the florist's?

KEN: She got the cards mixed up on the flowers. She sent one to a bride that read, 'With deepest sympathy', and one to a funeral that read, 'Hope you'll be happy in your new home.'

Very Silly Jokes

A very silly young girl called Veronica went to a friend's house for the evening. They ate a delicious meal, told each other all the latest gossip, watched their favourite TV programme, and played computer games. When the time came for Veronica to go home, there was a tremendous thunderstorm. Thunder rolled and crashed, the sky was split by lightning, and the rain poured down. Veronica shuddered.

'What's the matter?' asked her friend.

'I'm terrified of thunder,' admitted Veronica. 'I daren't go out in it.'

'That's all right,' said her friend. 'You can spend the night here.'

'Oh, I couldn't put you to all that trouble,' replied Veronica.

'It's no trouble,' said her friend. 'Do stay.'

'Are you sure?' asked Veronica.

'Absolutely,' answered her friend.

'Well, all right then,' said Veronica. 'But I'd better just nip home first and collect my nightie and toothbrush.'

Why did the man live under his bed?
Because he was a little potty.

How many legs does an ant have?
Two, same as an uncle.

TEACHER: If you had one pound, and you asked your mother for another pound, how much money would you have?
RYAN: **One pound.**
TEACHER: You don't know much about arithmetic.
RYAN: **You don't know much about my mother!**

Which airlines do teddies use?
British Bearways.

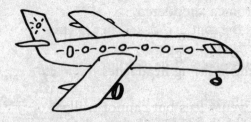

ADAM: How do you spell 'Ercules, Miss?
TEACHER: You mean Hercules?
ADAM: No, I've written the H already.

JIMMY: When my cousin lived in Australia he used to chase kangaroos on horses.
TIMMY: Fancy that! I didn't even know kangaroos could ride horses.

What's yellow and always points north?
A magnetic banana.

FATHER: How did you manage to get minus one in
your spelling test?
DENZIL: I spelt my name wrong too.

MRS BLACK: Will you join me in a cup of tea?
**MRS BROWN: Do you think there'll be room for both
of us?**

What's green and hairy and takes an aspirin?
A gooseberry with a headache.

Did you hear you can buy a new pill that's
half aspirin and half glue?
It's for curing splitting headaches.

What has twenty legs but cannot walk?
Ten pairs of trousers.

RUDY: What's the difference
between a sandwich, a bus and a
tube of glue?
TRUDIE: I don't know.
RUDY: Well, you can eat a sandwich but
you can't eat a bus.
**TRUDIE: Yes, but what about the
tube of glue?**
RUDY: Ah, I thought that was
where you'd get stuck.

How do you make a lemon drop?
Shake the tree hard.

LOCAL: What do you think of our village band?
VISITOR: I think it ought to be.
LOCAL: What do you mean 'it ought to be'?
VISITOR: It ought to be banned.

Why didn't the grape snore?
It didn't want to wake up the rest of the bunch.

What was the comedian's favourite supper?
Fish and quips.

Two men sat arguing in a railway carriage about whether the window should be open or closed.

The first said, 'If I don't have that window open, I shan't be able to breathe, and I shall suffocate.'

'Rubbish!' said the second. 'Of course you won't suffocate. On the other hand, if that window isn't closed, I shall get pneumonia from the cold draught.'

The argument went on and on, and the men were making so much noise with their raised voices that eventually the guard came to see what was happening. He listened to the argument for a while, wondering how to solve the problem. Eventually, another passenger in the carriage tapped him on the shoulder.

'Open the window for a while, and that will get rid of one of them,' he said. 'Then close it for a while, and that will get rid of the other. Then we can all have a bit of peace and quiet!'

A famous TV journalist went for a meal at a very well-known gourmet restaurant. As each course arrived, he savoured it and praised it rapturously to the waiter. When he had finished his dessert, the head waiter came and asked him if he had enjoyed his meal.

'It was absolutely first class,' said the journalist. 'I've never enjoyed a meal more. In fact, I'd very much like to meet your chef to tell him so personally.'

So the head waiter fetched the chef, and the journalist told him how much he had enjoyed each course of the meal.

'And what was your favourite dish?' asked the chef.

'I think, probably, the fish,' replied the journalist. 'The sauce was magnificent. I'd like to try and make it at home, I'm a bit of a cook myself. Tell me, what did you put into it?'

The chef smiled but shook his head. 'I'm afraid,' he answered, 'that good chefs, like good journalists, never reveal their sauces.'

How many potatoes can you carry in an empty bucket?
Only one, after that it isn't empty any more.

If a buttercup is yellow, what colour is a hiccup?
Burple.

JULES: Have you a blue shirt to match my eyes?
SHOP ASSISTANT: No, but we have some soft hats to match your head.

How can you make a bandstand?
Take away their chairs.

What did the man say when he walked into a bar?
'Ouch!'

Did you hear about the man who left his shoes at the cobbler's to be soled?
When he returned the next day the cobbler said he'd managed to get a couple of pounds for them.

CUSTOMER: A packet of birdseed, please.
SHOP ASSISTANT: Certainly, sir. How many birds have you got?
CUSTOMER: None, yet, I'm hoping to grow some.

KAREN: I bought a bottle of that new toilet water. It cost me twenty-five pounds.
SHARON: Twenty-five pounds! You should have come round to our house, you could have had water out of the toilet for free.

An American tourist was seeing the sights of London on an open-topped tour bus. Whenever the guide pointed out a historic site, such as Westminster Abbey, he'd say, 'Why, back home we could put up a building like that in a couple of weeks.'

The guide was getting pretty fed up, so when they passed the Tower of London, and the tourist asked, 'What's that building?', the guide replied, 'I don't know, it wasn't there yesterday.'

Another American tourist, a very large lady, was telling her friend about her attempts to lose weight. 'I lost thirty pounds when I was in Britain,' she said.

'Gee!' replied her friend. 'How much is that in dollars?'

Yet another American tourist was visiting Australia. The guide showed him Ayers Rock and asked what he thought of it.

'Very impressive,' said the tourist. 'But we've got much bigger rock formations back home.'

Then they went to Sydney, where the guide pointed out the amazing architecture of the Opera House.

'Sure,' said the tourist, 'but we've got even more amazing buildings in my city.'

Then they went to Bondi Beach. The guide said how beautiful it was, but the tourist said they had better beaches in his country.

On the way back to the hotel, they passed some kangaroos, which the guide pointed out. The tourist rubbed his chin. 'Mmm,' he muttered. 'I must admit, your grasshoppers are bigger than ours.'

JAKE: Er, Mum, you know that special dish you were always worried that I would break?
MUM: Yes. Why?
JAKE: Well, your worries are over.

MUM: I think there's a burglar downstairs. Are you awake?
DAD: No.

What do you call a camel with three humps?
Humphrey.

Why did a father and mother call both their sons Edward?
Because two Eds are better than one.

Three very old and rather deaf friends met one day in the street.
　'Windy, isn't it?' said the first.
　'No,' said the second, 'it's Thursday.'
　'So am I,' said the third. 'Let's find somewhere to have a cup of tea.'

Why can't a car play football?
Because it only has one boot.

A man was standing outside a tube station playing a violin when an old friend of his walked by.

'Hello, Jim,' said the friend. 'I'm sorry to see you in this predicament. Have you lost your job?'

Jim laughed. 'Oh, no, it's nothing like that. It's just that my wife won't let me practise in the house.'

'Oh, I see,' said the friend, relieved. 'Do you usually play by ear?'

'Not often,' replied Jim. 'I usually play over there.'

Two other old friends bumped into each other for the first time in over twenty years.

'Well, hello, Dave,' said Dick. 'Great to see you. How's life been treating you?'

'To be honest,' replied Dave, 'not too well. Two years ago my wife ran off with my best friend. Last year my son got expelled from school because he was so naughty. This year my daughter had to have an operation, I fell down some steps and broke my leg, my car got written off in an accident, and the gas cooker blew up and wrecked our kitchen.'

'Oh dear,' said Dick. 'That doesn't sound too good. How's your work going? What are you doing now?'

'Well,' said Dave, 'I sell lucky charms.'

JIM: How much do you earn?
TIM: Oh, roughly £300 a week.
JIM: What do you mean, 'roughly'?
TIM: Well, when I smooth it out it's more like £150.

BUS PASSENGER: Is this bus going to Clapham?
BUS CONDUCTOR: Only if they perform really well.

If a straight line is the shortest distance between two points, what is a beeline?
The shortest distance between two buzz stops.

JENNY: They say money talks.
KENNY: Mine doesn't. It goes without saying.

JOSS: Can you lend me a tenner for a week, old dear?
ROSS: Who's the weak old dear?

DEBBIE: My little brother has a new hobby.
TEDDY: What's that?
DEBBIE: He collects worms.
TEDDY: What does he do with them?
DEBBIE: He presses them.

What happened when the potato died?
There was a huge turnip at his funeral.

TEACHER: Today we are going to study Kipling. Do you like Kipling, Brian?
BRIAN: I don't know, miss, I've never kippled.

What can you do if you get locked out of your house?
Sing until you get the right key.

Where do loonies do their shopping?
Insanesburys.

How do you make a Mexican chilli?
Take him to Siberia.

A mouse went to a music shop and asked to buy a mouth organ. The shop assistant looked at the mouse in amazement.

'In all the years I've worked in this shop we've never had a mouse asking for a mouth organ until today, and you're the second one who's been in this morning,' she exclaimed.

'Ah,' replied the mouse. 'The first one would have been 'ar Monica.'

How can you tell the difference between a tin of
sardines and a tin of tuna fish?
Read the label.

What did the loony call his pet tiger?
Spot.

Did you hear what happened when a man bought a
paper shop?
It blew away.

TEACHER: Do you know the Lord's Prayer?
**SILLY SAMMY: Is that what they say at
the cricket ground when they don't want
it to rain?**

Why did the boy keep his
socks on when paddling
at the seaside?
The water was cold.

What pantomime is about a
cat in a chemist's shop?
Puss in Boots.

TRAFFIC WARDEN: Why did you park your car here,
sir?
DRIVER: Because the sign says, 'Fine for parking.'

A man was walking down the road dragging behind him a large turnip on a dog lead. Several people looked at him strangely, though no one said anything until a kindly old lady came along. Poor thing! she thought. He must be a bit mad, but I'll play along with him.

So she walked up to the man, bent down and patted the turnip, and said, 'What a nice little dog you've got.'

The man gave her a very odd look. 'That's not a dog, it's a turnip,' he said.

'Oh, right,' said the lady, and walked on, scratching her head.

When she'd gone, the man looked at the turnip and said, 'That fooled her, didn't it, Fido?'

How do you start a rice pudding race?
Sago.

How do you start a bear race?
Say, 'Ready, teddy, go!'

Two men met at a conference for salespeople in the catering industry. 'What do you sell?' one man asked the other.
'Pepper,' replied the second one.
'So do I,' said the first. 'Shake?'

DEREK: I haven't slept for days.
ERIC: Why not?
DEREK: I sleep at night.

JIMMY: What kind of soup is this?
MUM: It's bean soup.
JIMMY: I don't care what it's been, what is it now?

What lives in the sea and is good at adding up?
An octoplus.

How do you get two whales in a Mini?
Over the Severn Bridge.

What didn't Adam and Eve have that everybody else has?
Parents!

What's red, covered in pips, and drinks from the wrong side of a glass?
A strawberry with hiccups.

How can you tell which end of a worm is its head?
Tickle its middle and see which end smiles.

'I went to an art exhibition last week.'
'Gaugin?'
'No, once was enough.'

It Pays to Advertise

FOR SALE: Sailing boat, moored Southampton. Owner retired and no further use.

LOST IN MARKET: Octagonal lady's gold watch.

FOR SALE: Bungalow, two bedrooms, nice garden. All reasonable offers rejected.

WANTED: Lady to wash, iron and milk two cows.

LOST: Antique pendant depicting the Virgin and Child in Covent Garden on Saturday night.

ROOM TO LET: Suitable for two ladies, use of kitchen or two gentlemen.

HOUSE FOR SALE: Three bedrooms, kitchen, living room, bathroom, separate WC two miles outside Guildford.

FOR SALE: Set of bagpipes, or swap for shotgun.

FOAM-RUBBER CUSHIONS for sale, rock-bottom prices.

LADY seeks cleaning, four days a week, or would divide in two.

POODLE PUPPIES FOR SALE: Sire Champion Foxearth Freddie, dam well bred.

BRIGHTON: B & B, comfortable rooms, good food, germs moderate.

1955 ROLLS-ROYCE hearse for sale. Good condition, original body.

FRENCH WIDOWS made to order. Send for details.

FLAT TO LET: Two rooms, k and b, £100 a week, rats included.

MG SPORTS CAR for sale, one lady owner with soft top.

FLAT REQUIRED to rent by professional couple expecting quiet baby.

LADIES: Try our super-sheer tights. Intended for evening wear but so comfortable many ladies wear nothing else.

CENTRAL LAUNDERETTE: Leave your clothes here, ladies, and spend the morning shopping.

EARS PIERCED while you wait.

FORD ESCORT for sale, one owner, green in colour.

LOST: Four £5 notes in High Street on Saturday, sentimental value.

WE EXCHANGE EVERYTHING – washing machines, TVs, videos, CD players – bring your wife and get the deal of your life!

FOR SALE: Three-bra electric fire.

FOR SALE: Baby cooker, good condition.

ANTIQUE porcelain dinner service for sale by lady only slightly cracked.

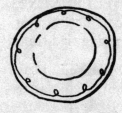

YOUNG MAN, 25, non-driver, would like to accompany similar on car tour of France.

FOR SALE: Fish-and-chip fryer, made from chip-resistant enamel.

CLEANER required for small officers, ten hours per week.

TO LET: Blackpool beach, cosy bungalow with sea through lounge.

PORTRAITS: Children and pets executed at your own home.

GENUINE STRADI-VARIUS VIOLIN for sale, good condition, almost new.

WANTED: Home help – to live in with elderly gentleman to hell with the cooking and cleaning.

LONELY HEARTS CLUB: Don't be lonely – we have lots of good fiends waiting to meet you.

WANTED: Person to wash dishes and a waitress for new restaurant opening soon.

SALLY'S RESTAURANT:
Please note we now serve
Sunday lunches seven days
a week.

WANTED: Man to stick
on wallpaper.

EAT AT JACK'S CAFE –
where good food is an
unexpected pleasure.

BRIAN'S BUTCHERS –
best Scotch beef from
Wales.

HOUSE FOR SALE – four
bedrooms, lounge, dining
room, bathroom, fitted
kitchen with plumber in
washing machine and
dishwasher.

LOST: Jack Russell terrier,
white with black ears, tail
and feet missing since last
Sunday.

EXPERIENCED baby-
sister available.

**A SELECTION OF
BEAUTIFUL RINGS** by
mail order. State size or
enclose string tied round
finger.

**WEDDING DRESS FOR
SALE:** Cream silk, size 14,
only worn twice.

WANTED: pianist, both
upright and grand.

THREE-PIECE SUITE for
sale. Sofa turns into bed
covered in yellow mustard.

Fearsome Families

BILL: Dad, a man called while you were out.
DAD: Did he have a bill?
BILL: No, just an ordinary nose like everyone else has.

DAD: What did I say I'd do if I caught you stealing the strawberries again?
BEN: That's funny, I can't remember either.

JULIE: What are they going to call your new little brother?
JENNY: Well, they're thinking of naming him after his father.
JULIE: What, you mean they're going to call him Dad?

DAD: Who gave you that black eye?
CHARLIE: Nobody gave it me, I had to fight for it.

DAD: Have you been fighting again? You seem to have lost your front teeth!
DAN: No I haven't, they're in my pocket.

JANE: Do you know what I'm going to give you for Christmas?
MUM: No, what?
JANE: A nice glass vase.
MUM: But I've already got a nice glass vase.
JANE: No you haven't, I just dropped it!

One dark and stormy night little Freddie's mum tiptoed up to his bedroom in case he was frightened of the thunder and lightning.

'Are you all right, Freddie?' she called round the door.

'Yes, thanks, Mum,' he replied. 'Is Dad fiddling about with the telly again?'

AUNTIE BET: You're very quiet today, Samantha.
SAMANTHA: That's because Mum gave me fifty pence not to say anything about your bald patch.

MUM: Are you ready yet, Kylie? Have you put your shoes on?
KYLIE: Yes, Mum, all except one.

A farmer walked past his orchard and caught sight of a small boy up in the branches dropping apples into a bag.

'Oi!' he yelled. 'Come down here this minute or I'll go and tell your father!'

'You can tell him now,' answered the lad cheekily. 'He's up here with me.'

'Everything in our house works perfectly.'
'My mum says that's because your dad never does any DIY.'

SIMON: May I practise this song on the piano?
MUM: Yes, but wash your hands first, they're filthy.
SIMON: That's OK, I'll only play on the black

notes.

Nigel was a very naughty little boy. One morning, when his mother was trying to work on the household accounts, he really tried her patience. He kept running round the house, up and down the stairs, making a lot of noise, charging in and out of the room in which she was trying to work. So she told him to go and play in the garden, but he immediately tried to climb a tree, and managed to rip his trousers. This was the last straw, as all his other trousers were in the wash.

'Nigel!' yelled his mother. 'Take off those trousers, go upstairs and either play your computer games or read a book until lunchtime. I'll mend your trousers so you can put them on again, but I don't want to hear or see you until lunch is ready.'

For a while, the house was quiet, and Nigel's mother got on with the job of mending his trousers. Then she heard a noise coming up from the cellar.

'You bad boy!' she shouted. 'Are you running about down there with no trousers on?'

'No, madam,' came a voice. 'I'm reading the gas meter.'

MUM: You are in a mess, what have you been doing?
TARA: I fell down in a puddle, Mum.
MUM: What, in those new white jeans?
TARA: Well, I didn't have time to change.

SURESH: Mum, will you wash my face, please?
MUM: Why can't you wash it yourself?
SURESH: Because then I'll have to get my hands

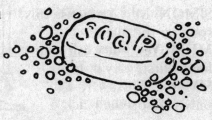

wet and they're not dirty.

'Dad, my friend Harry says I look just like you.'

'Does he? And what do you say?'

'I don't say anything, he's bigger than me!'

Sammy's teacher wrote a letter to Sammy's father complaining about Sammy's behaviour in class. 'What's all this?' asked his Dad. 'Your teacher says here that it's impossible to teach you anything!'

'I told you he was hopeless,' replied Sammy.

MUM: Why are you crying?

EDDIE: I trapped my finger in the door.

MUM: When did you do that?

EDDIE: About half an hour ago.

MUM: I didn't hear you crying then.

EDDIE: No, I thought you were out.

GRANDMA: I wouldn't slide down the banisters like that if I were you, Adam.

ADAM: Oh, how would you slide down them, Gran?

Gran bought a new, rear-engined car. She was very proud of it, and one day went round to see her old friend Brenda to take her out for a ride.

The two ladies drove through the countryside, heading for a seaside town, where they stopped for lunch. They then went for a walk, did some shopping, and had tea.

'It's getting late,' said Brenda. 'We'd better head for home.'

So they set off, but after a few miles the car broke down. 'Oh dear,' said Brenda. She got out of the car and opened its bonnet. 'Help!' she exclaimed. 'Did you know you've lost your engine?'

'Don't worry, dear,' said Gran reassuringly. 'I've got another one in the boot.'

MUM: It was kind of you to let your sister have first go on your skates.
BEN: That's all right, Mum, I thought I'd let her find out if the ice is thick enough.

MUM: Why did you put a mouse in your sister's bed?
DENNIS: Because I couldn't find a frog.

MUM: Did you say 'thank you' to Mrs Evans for inviting you to the party?
JIM: No.
MUM: Why not?
JIM: Well, the boy in front of me said 'thank you' and Mrs Evans said 'Don't mention it' so I didn't.

WAYNE: What was Snow White's brother called?
JAYNE: I don't know.
WAYNE: Egg White. Get the yolk?

GARY: My sister's gone on a crash diet.

GABY: Is that why she looks such a wreck?
JASON: Do you have a good memory for faces?
DAD: Yes. Why?
JASON: Because I've just broken your shaving mirror.

MUM: What happened to your nose? It's all red and swollen.
CHARLIE: I was smelling a brose.
MUM: You mean a rose. There's no B in 'rose'.
CHARLIE: There was in this one!

GRANDAD: I didn't enjoy supper much last night. Can we have something I can get my teeth into tonight?
GRANDMA: Certainly, here's a glass of water.

GINA: My sister went to a beauty parlour.
TINA: Did she think they could perform miracles?

'My cousin's been at university for years.'
'Yes, I'd heard he has more degrees than a thermometer.'

LARRY: I can trace my ancestry right back down our family tree.
HARRY: Back to when your ancestors lived in it?

BERNIE: One of my ancestors died at Waterloo.
ERNIE: Really? Which platform?

AUNTIE: What are you going to give your little sister for Christmas?
ANDY: I don't know. Last year I gave her chickenpox.

'Does your mother lie about her age?'
'Not exactly. She says she's the same age as Dad, and

then lies about his age!'
GRANDSON: Grandad, were you on Noah's ark?
GRANDAD: No, of course not!
GRANDSON: Then how did you manage not to be drowned?

'My grandad's wonderful for his age. He's ninety-five and hasn't a grey hair on his head.'
'Really?'
'Yes, he's completely bald.'

'When my grandad has a cold he buys a bottle of whisky and in no time it's gone.'
'The cold or the whisky?'

'My grandfather says he believes in a balanced diet. He keeps a bottle of whisky in each hand.'

'My grandfather lived to be a hundred and never used glasses.'
'Lots of people drink straight from the bottle these days.'

MUM: You're taking a long time writing that letter to your gran.
LISA: Well, she can't see very well, so I'm writing very

slowly.

GRANDMA: If you wait here for a few minutes and watch, Maggie, you'll see the cuckoo come out of the cuckoo clock.

MAGGIE: I'd rather see Grandad come out of the grandfather clock.

LITTLE BILLY: Grandad, can you do frog impressions?

GRANDAD: No, why do you ask?

LITTLE BILLY: Because Dad keeps saying we'll have a lot of money when you croak.

Why did Grandma put wheels on her rocking chair?
Because she wanted to rock and roll.

'There's one thing you can say about your father, he puts in a good day's work. Unfortunately it takes him a month to do it.'

'Your father is out of this world.'
'My mum often wishes he were.'

'My dad says he's welcome in all the best homes.'
'Of course he is, he's a plumber.'

'My dad's in hospital.'
'Oh dear, what happened?'
'He climbed the tree to pick some
apples for Mum to make a pie for
dinner, and fell out of it and
broke his leg.'
'What did your mum do?'
'Opened a tin of peaches.'

Mrs Feather asked her husband if they could have a
video recorder. 'I'm afraid we can't afford one,' he
replied. Next day Mrs Feather arrived home with a
large box containing – a video recorder!

'How on earth did you find the money to buy that?'
asked her husband.

'Oh, it was easy,' replied his wife. 'I sold the TV.'

Mrs and Mrs Scuttle and their son Sammy were having lunch in a restaurant. When they had finished, Mr Scuttle called the waiter over.

'My son has left a lot of meat on his plate,' he said. 'May we have a bag to take it home for the dog?'

'Hey,' said Sammy, 'that's cool. I didn't know we had a dog.'

Dad had a headache, and got very annoyed with young Adam, who came tearing down the stairs making a great deal of noise. 'Adam!' he roared, 'you sound like a herd of elephants! Will you please come down the stairs more quietly? Go back up and come down without making all that noise!'

After a few minutes' silence, Adam walked into the living room, where his father was sitting. 'That's better,' said his dad. 'Now, please come down the stairs as quietly as that in future.'

'Fine,' shrugged Adam. 'I slid down the banister.'

'Mum got a puppy for my brother.'
'Wow, I wish I could do a swap like that!'

'My Dad can lift a gorilla with one hand.'
'I don't believe it!'
'Show me a gorilla with one hand and I'll prove it!'

'And what did your father say when you were sent to prison?'
'Hello, son.'

106

MUM: You mustn't fight Johnny. You must learn to count up to ten before you lose your temper.
JIMMY: I did, but Johnny's mum only told him to count up to five and he hit me first.

A young curate was walking down the street when he came across two boys fighting. He managed to pull them apart, and said firmly, 'You shouldn't fight, God teaches us to love our enemies.'

'But he's not my enemy,' yelled both boys together, 'he's my brother!'

TOMMY: Dad, what's a weapon?
DAD: It's something you fight with.
TOMMY: You mean like Mum?

What happened when the wife told her husband to go to blazes?
He joined the fire brigade.

DAD: What did you learn in school today?
LAUREN: That the sums you did for my homework were wrong!

'Did your mum take you to meet your dad at the airport?'
'Oh no, he's lived with us for years!'
MUM: You're such a naughty boy, Ben. If you don't

stop misbehaving I shall call a policeman.
BEN: If you do, I'll tell him we don't have a TV licence.

LILY: Sisters are brighter than brothers, you know.
BILLY: Really? I never knew that.
LILY: See what I mean?

DON: Your sister's spoilt, isn't she?
RON: No, it's just that horrible perfume she wears.

MUM: How many times must I tell you not to fight? You must learn to give and take.
RYAN: But I did. I took his football and gave him a black eye.

JOHNNY: Does your mum cook by gas or electricity?
DONNY: I don't know. I've never tried to cook her.

AUNT: And what is Gilly going to be when she's passed all her exams?
MUM: An old-age pensioner.

A young father was walking along the road with a screaming child in a pushchair. As he walked he was muttering, 'Calm down, Jake, calm down, everything will be all right.'

A passing granny smiled at him. 'You're doing very well trying to soothe your son,' she said. She peered at the pushchair and said, 'What's the matter, Jake?'

'He's not Jake,' said the young father, 'I am!'

LAURA: Why have you got grey hair, Mum?
MUM: I expect it's because I have to worry so much about you.
LAURA: You must have made Grandma worry ever such a lot then!

NEIGHBOUR: Is your new baby sister here to stay?
SUSIE: I think so, she's taken all her clothes off.

What kind of babies live in the sea?
Buoys.

DAD: Our new baby
is the image of me.
NEIGHBOUR:
Never mind,
as long as
he's healthy.

Haunting Tales

What were the aristocratic ghost's favourite pastimes?
Haunting, shooting and fishing.

What happened when the ghost went into a cow shed?
The cows produced milkshakes.

What kind of ghost works for the police force?
An in-spectre.

How does a ghost get through a locked door?
He uses a skeleton key.

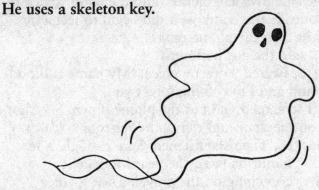

BUTLER: Excuse me, sir, there's a ghost waiting in the hall.
LORD LOTTADOSH: Tell him I can't see him.

What did the ghost call the skeleton?
Bonehead.

What do you call a sailor's ghost?
A sea-ghoul.

What do ghosts like for dinner?
Ghoulash.

Where do ghosts go on holiday?
Lake Eerie.

How do ghosts cross the Channel?
By hovercraft.

What do ghosts like on their apple pie?
Evaporated milk.

A young woman went to stay in a house that was
supposed to be haunted. She didn't believe in such
things, so she was not afraid. However, as night drew
on and the shadows lengthened, and the wind sighed in
the trees outside the window, it did begin to feel a bit
spooky. Just then the phone rang.

'Hello,' said the girl hesitantly.

'Hello,' answered a creepy voice. 'My name is Blood-
stained Hand and I'm coming to get you!'

The girl screamed and put the phone down. She shot
the bolts on the door and ran up to her room, which
she also locked. Then she listened. Sure enough, a few
moments later, she heard footsteps
crunching on the gravel. Then a voice
called out, 'My name is Blood-stained
Hand and I'm coming to get you!'

The girl screamed again and locked
herself in the wardrobe. She heard the front
door open, even though she'd locked it, and
heavy footsteps coming up the stairs. She
pushed herself further into the
wardrobe, but kept an eye on its
keyhole, through which she could see

her bedroom. The voice came again. 'My name is Blood-stained Hand and I'm coming to get you!'

She trembled with fear. She saw her bedroom door open very, very slowly, and a hideous creature slouched into the room, its claw-like hand dripping blood on to the carpet. It reached out for the wardrobe door, repeating, 'My name is Blood-stained Hand and I'm coming to get you!'

'W-w-what do you want?' whispered the terror-stricken girl.

'Do you think you could bandage my hand, please?' it answered.

BRIDGET: If you don't believe in ghosts, how come you won't sleep in the haunted house?
BRIAN: I might be wrong!

Who writes ghost jokes?
A crypt writer.

Where in the graveyard would you find a ghost?
At the spirit level.

What's a ghost's favourite tree?
A ceme-tree.

What do ghosts wear for reading?
Spooktacles.

How do ghosts count?
'One, boo, three, four, five, six, seven, hate, nine, frighten!'

Where does a ghost train stop?
At a manifestation.

How do ghosts keep fit?
They exorcise at the gym.

Where do ghosts go
swimming?
In the Dead Sea.

What did the baby ghost
call his parents?
Deady and mummy.

Which ghost was friends with the three bears?
Ghouldilocks.

What do you call a drunken ghost?
A methylated spirit.

A teacher ghost was explaining a complicated
mathematical problem to her pupils. 'Now,' she said,
'did you all understand that, or shall I go through it
again?'

What did the mother ghost say to her son who didn't
always tell the truth?
**'It's no use trying to fool me, you know I can see right
through you.'**

What do ghosts like for breakfast?
Dreaded wheat.

What do Italian ghosts like to eat?
Spookhetti.

Which ghost was once president of France?
Charles de Ghoul.

FIRST GHOST: What's the difference between a sheet
and a person?
SECOND GHOST: **One I wear, the other I was.**

What wears a sheet and lights up?
An electric ghost.

What do you find in the cellar of a haunted house?
Whines and spirits.

What did the
mother ghost say
to her unruly
child?
**'Only spook
when you're
spooken to.'**

FIONA: I think I met a
ghost last night.
FINLAY: **Did it speak?**
FIONA: Yes.
FINLAY: **What did it say?**
FIONA: I don't know, I don't understand dead
languages.

FIRST GHOST: You look tired.
SECOND GHOST: **Yes, I'm dead on my feet.**

What happened when two ghosts ran in the 200-metre
race?
It was a dead heat.

Where did the lady ghost part her hair?
In the dead centre.

How did the ghost work out his income tax?
By dead reckoning.

What did the lady ghost put on her face?
Vanishing cream.

Why did the lonely spook go to the graveyard?
Because there was always somebody there.

Al A. Tremble, a timid young man, was driving home
one wild and stormy night. The rain was lashing down,
thunder rumbled ominously, and every so often great
sheets of lightning lit up the sky. Al was very frightened,
and longed to be safe in his house. But fate was against
him. As he approached a village church, his car broke
down and he couldn't get it to start again.

  He didn't relish the idea of spending the night in his
car, but he suddenly had a brainwave. 'Aunty Joan lives
in this village,' he thought. 'I could go to her house and
stay there.' He looked around him to get his bearings. 'I
think she lives just the other side of this church. I'll nip
through the graveyard, it will be quicker than going
round by the road and I shan't get as wet.'

So he set off. It was very creepy in the graveyard. The wind made the trees creak, and the lightning lit up old, mouldering headstones. Al shuddered. Then he heard the tapping. It was quite regular, 'Tap, tap, tap, tap, tap.' It would stop for a moment, then start again, 'Tap, tap, tap, tap, tap.' It seemed to come from the far side of one of the headstones.

Poor Al was terrified, but he had to find out what it was. He crept forward and peered into the darkness, and there was a white-sheeted figure holding a hammer and a chisel, tapping away at the stone.

'Wh-a-a-t are you doing?' stammered Al.

'I'm correcting the headstone,' replied the figure. 'They spelt my name wrong.'

Who looks after a haunted house?
A skeleton staff.

What do you call a
skeleton who goes out
in the snow without a
hat on?
A numbskull.

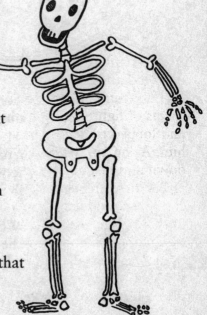

How did the skeleton know it
was going to snow?
He could feel it in his bones.

How do you make a skeleton
laugh?
Tickle its funny bone.

What do you call a skeleton that
sits around all day?
Lazybones.

What did the silly skeleton say when he called on his friend?
'Hello, is anybody home?'

What's a skeleton's favourite vegetable?
Marrow.

Why do skeletons like drinking milk?
It's good for their bones.

What did the skeleton put on his tea table?
Bone china cups and saucers.

What do skeletons do for charity?
Sell rattle tickets.

Why did the skeleton's teeth chatter?
He was chilled to the marrow.

What *is* a skeleton?
Someone who wears his insides outside.

What did the skeleton say when he was cross with his friend?
'I've a bone to pick with you.'

Why didn't the skeleton go to the disco?
Because he had nobody to dance with.

Why did the skeleton gardener complain?
Because he had to work his fingers to the bone.

Why wouldn't the skeleton take up parachuting?
He just didn't have the guts.

What did the barber say to the skeleton?
'You're getting a bit thin on top.'

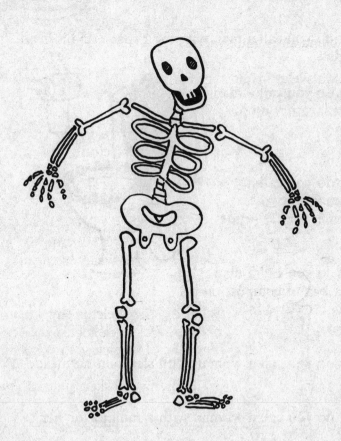

What Do You Call . . . ?

What do you call a man with a spade on his head?
Doug.

What do you call a man without a spade on his head?
Douglas.

What do you call a man
with a lavatory on his
head?
John.

What do you call a
woman with two
lavatories on her head?
Lulu.

What do you call a man
with a bag of compost on his
head?
Pete.

What do you call a woman with slates on her head?
Ruth.

What do you call a woman with a radiator on her
head?
Anita.

What do you call a man with a smudge on his nose?
Mark.

What do you call a man with a carpet on his head?
Matt.

What do you call a man with a telescope on his head?
Luke.

What do you call a woman with a frog on her head?
Lily.

What do you call a man with a wig on his head?
Aaron.

What do you call a woman with a diary on her head?
Tamara.

What do you call a woman with a radio on her head?
Alison.

What do you call a man with a seagull on his head?
Cliff.

What do you call a man with a large black and blue
mark on his head?
Bruce.

What do you call a man with scratches on his head?
Claude.

What do you call a man with a crane on his head?
Derek.

What do you call a man with a
grating on his head?
Dwayne.

What do you call a woman
with a cat on her head?
Kitty.

What do you call a man with a
plank on his head?
Edward.

What do you call a woman with a weight on one side
of her head?
Eileen.

What do you call a woman with a map on her head?
Wanda.

What do you call a woman with a storm on her head?
Gail.

What do you call a woman with a handshake on her
head?
Greta.

What do you call a man with a pot of paint on his
head?
Hugh.

What do you call a man with a car on his head?
Jack.

What do you call a man with a signpost on his head?
Miles.

What do you call a man with an invoice on his head?
Owen.

What do you call a man with a paper bag on his head?
Russell.

What do you call a man with very
little hair on his head?
Shaun.

What do you call a man
with sunken ships on
his head?
Rex.

What do you call a woman with a tortoise on her head?
Shelley.

What do you call a man with rabbits on his head?
Warren.

What do you call a man with a car number plate on his head?
Reg.

What do you call a woman with a Christmas tree on her head?
Carol.

What do you call a woman with jewels on her head?
Gemma.

What do you call a man with a landscape on his head?
Glen.

What do you call a man with a knight in armour on his head?
Lance.

What do you call a man with a burglar on his head?
Robin.

What do you call a woman
with a parrot on
her head?
Polly.

What do you call a woman with a slot machine on her
head?
Penny.

What do you call a woman with a toy on her head?
Dolly.

What do you call a man with pound coins on his head?
Stirling.

Getting the Pip

What do lemons enjoy watching on TV?
Top of the Pips.

What's a vampire's favourite fruit?
A blood orange.

Why did the banana go to the doctor's?
It wasn't peeling very well.

How do you make a banana split?
Cut it in half.

What's purple and lies in the sea off Europe?
Grape Britain.

JAMIE: Why are you eating that banana with its skin on?
MAMIE: I know what's inside.

Why aren't grapes ever lonely?
Because they hang around in bunches.

What happened to the man who stole a lorryload of plums?
He was put into custardy.

What did the grape say when the elephant trod on it?
Nothing, it just gave out a little w(h)ine.

Which purple fruit ruled the world?
Alexander the Grape.

What is a raisin?
A very worried grape.

What's it called when a grape hits a plum?
A fruit punch.

Why did the man eat a hundred plums a day?
He was plum crazy!

What do you do with a plum that leaks?
Call a plumber.

What sits in a fruit bowl and cries for help?
A damson in distress.

What's covered in custard and
complains a lot?
Apple grumble.

What do you call a Welsh apple?
A Taffy apple.

Why are apple seeds like gateposts?
Because they propagate.

What did the boy say to the angry farmer when he was
caught climbing up an apple tree?
**'One of the apples fell down and I was putting it back
for you.'**

What's green and hairy and out of breath?
A gooseberry riding a bicycle up a hill.

What's green and hairy and red?
An embarrassed gooseberry.

What's blue and hairy?
A gooseberry holding its breath.

On which side does a gooseberry have the most hairs?
The outside.

How can you tell a gooseberry from an elephant?
A gooseberry is green.

What's round, orange and can't sit down?
A seatless satsuma.

What should you do with a green banana?
Try to teach it something.

What should you do with a blue banana?
Try to cheer it up.

What did one chick say to his brother when they found an orange in their nest?
'Look what Mama laid.'

What do you call a fat pumpkin?
A plumpkin.

What did one raspberry say to the other?
'How did we get into this jam?'

What is a prickly pear?
Two hedgehogs.

What is green, is found in a salad and plays snooker?
A cue-cumber.

What's green on the inside and yellow on the outside?
A cucumber disguised as a banana.

What kind of shoes can you make out of two banana skins?
A pair of slippers.

What do you get if you cross a box of dates with a lot of famous people?
A history lesson.

Milly and Minnie, two very old ladies who lived in a cottage deep in the country, were taking their very first trip on a train. Milly's niece took them to the station in her car, and saw them on to the train. She gave them some bananas to eat on the journey.

The two old ladies had never eaten bananas before, and after a while they began to feel hungry. So Milly peeled two bananas and handed one to her friend.

Just as Minnie took a bite out of her banana, the train entered a tunnel, and everything went dark.

'Help!' screamed Minnie.

'What's the matter?' asked her friend.

'Have you tried your banana yet?' asked Minnie.

'No,' replied Milly.

'Well, don't,' answered Minnie. 'I took one bite and went blind.'

JIM: How did you get that lump on your head?
TIM: Someone threw tomatoes at me.
JIM: But tomatoes are soft and squashy!
TIM: These weren't, they were inside a tin.

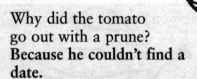

Why did the tomato go out with a prune?
Because he couldn't find a date.

SILLY BOY AT GREENGROCER'S: Who's in charge of the nuts?
GREENGROCER: Hang on a minute, sonny, and I'll come and help you.

SILLY CUSTOMER AT THE GREENGROCER'S: I'd like half a kilo of mixed nuts, please, with not too many coconuts.

What nut sounds like a sneeze?
A cashew.

What kind of nut has no shell?
A doughnut.

What did the peanut report to the police?
That he'd been assaulted.

How do you make a fresh peach punch?
Give her boxing lessons.

Does an apple a day keep the doctor away?
It does if your aim is good enough!

If an apple a day does keep the doctor away, what does an onion a day do?
Keeps everyone away!

JAKE: I live on onions alone.
JACK: **I'm not surprised you're alone!**

What's worse than biting into an apple and finding a maggot?
Biting into an apple and

finding half a maggot!
What's an apricot?
What a baby monkey sleeps in.

What is rhubarb?
Embarrassed celery.

A gardener was wheeling a barrowload of manure when
his neighbour spotted him.

'What are you going to do with that manure?' asked
the neighbour.

'Put it on my rhubarb,' replied the gardener.

'Really?' exclaimed the neighbour. 'I put custard on
mine!'

What's the difference between a
gardener and a snooker player?
**One minds his peas, the other
minds his cues.**

How many peas are there in a pint?
Just one!

How can you calculate the colour of a
lettuce?
By using a greengauge.

Where did the baby lettuce come from?
The stalk brought it.

Andy worked on a building site, and at lunchtime sat down with his workmates to eat his sandwiches. He took one out of his pack, looked at it and sighed. 'Oh dear, cheese and tomato sandwiches. I don't really like them, but I'm so hungry I expect I'll have to eat them.'

The following day when he opened his sandwiches, he again had cheese and tomato, and again he muttered about how he didn't like them.

When the same thing happened on the third day, one of his workmates said to him, 'If you don't like cheese and tomato sandwiches, why don't you ask your wife to make you something else?'

'That wouldn't make any difference,' said Andy. 'She doesn't make my sandwiches, I do.'

Why was the tomato red?
Because it spotted the salad dressing.

What's the difference between a slimy lettuce and a miserable song?
One's a bad salad, the other a sad ballad.

How can eating fruit make you put on weight?
If you eat a plum and swallow its centre you'll gain a stone!

What do you get if you cross a banana with a bell?
A fruit that can peel itself.

What's yellow, washable and doesn't need ironing?
A drip-dry banana.

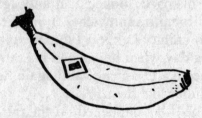

What's yellow and can write?
A ballpoint banana.

What's yellow and lights up?
An electric banana.

What's yellow and goes bang, bang, bang, bang?
A four-door banana.

What does a banana do when it's raining?
Gets wet.

What's a banana skin used for?
Holding the banana together.

What did one banana say to the other?
Nothing, bananas can't talk.

Cracking Good Jokes!

ROSS: I heard a new joke yesterday. Did I tell it to you?
FLOSS: Is it funny?
ROSS: Yes.
FLOSS: Then you didn't.

Bill and Ben were talking about the story of Jonah and the whale.

'Do you think it's true?' asked Bill. 'Do you think Jonah really was swallowed by a whale?'

'I don't know,' replied Ben. 'When I get to heaven I'll ask him.'

'But suppose he's not in heaven,' continued Bill.

'Then *you* can ask him,' answered Ben.

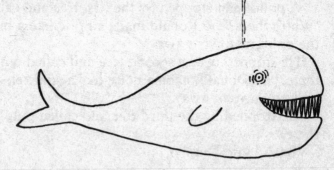

The children from Katie's school had been to a special service in the local church. They sang hymns, said their prayers, listened to readings, and heard the vicar preach a sermon about where humans came from and what would be their ultimate destiny. He used the Biblical sentence, 'Dust thou art, and unto dust thou shalt return.'

Katie was fascinated by this, and pondered on it on her way home. When she arrived, she went up to her room, but rushed downstairs a few moments later.

'Mum!' she cried, 'Come and look!'

'What's the matter, Katie?' asked her mum.

'There's someone under my bed,' answered Katie, 'and I don't know if they're coming or going!'

Ronald, Donald and Dumbo were on the run from the police. They ran into a forest, and each climbed up a tree.

A policeman stopped by the first tree and called out, 'Who's there?' So Ronald made a noise like a bird, and the policeman went away.

He stopped by the second tree and called out, 'Who's there?' So Donald made a noise like a squirrel, and the policeman went away.

He stopped by the third tree and called out, 'Who's there?'

'Baaa,' said Dumbo.

A famous pianist used to spend two hours every day practising, and during this time he would not be disturbed, no matter what happened. He had a housekeeper, and he gave her very strict instructions about this. He wouldn't answer the phone; he wouldn't see visitors.

One day, a man came to the door and said he needed to see the pianist urgently. 'I'm sorry,' said the housekeeper, 'but I'm afraid he is out.'

'I don't believe you,' said the visitor. 'I heard him playing as I came up to the door.'

'I'm afraid you are mistaken,' replied the housekeeper. 'That was me, dusting the piano keys.'

Why did the dumbo have his sundial floodlit?
So he could tell the time by it at night.

A policeman was interviewing a man who'd been in a motoring accident.

'And did you cause the accident?' the policeman asked.

'No,' replied the man. 'It was the other driver, a red-haired man driving a Ford Escort with a small moustache.'

GILLY: How did you cut your hand?
TILLY: I thought the window was open but I discovered it was closed when I put my hand through it.

MAMIE: I had bad eyesight until I was nine years old.
JAMIE: What happened then?
MAMIE: I had my fringe cut.

The young curate rushed up to the priest. 'Father, what shall I do?' he gasped. 'There's an old man with a long white beard sitting in the church and he says he's God!'

'Keep an eye on him,' replied the priest. 'And try to look busy.'

CUSTOMER: I'd like a haircut, please.
BARBER: Certainly, sir, which one?

Try this on a friend:
YOU: Adam and Eve and Pinch Me went down to the sea to bathe, Adam and Eve both got drowned, who do you think was saved?
FRIEND: Pinch Me.
It's up to you whether you do so or not!

St Peter was on duty at the gates of heaven when two astronauts rang the bell. St Peter greeted them. 'Good evening, gentlemen,' he said. 'If you'd like to come and sit in the waiting room we'll just check through your files and see if you are eligible to enter heaven.'

'Oh, sir, we don't want to come in just yet,' said the first astronaut.

'You don't?' asked St Peter. 'Then why did you ring the bell?'

'Please, sir,' said the second astronaut, 'may we have our spaceship back?'

Where were tomatoes first fried?
In Greece.

BOSS: Your work is a disgrace, Perkins. How do you manage to make so many mistakes in one day?
PERKINS: I get here early, sir.

Another boss was interviewing a job applicant. 'You'll get £200 a week when you start, and another £100 a week in a year's time.'
'Right,' said the man. 'I'll come back in a year's time.'

BOSS: Why do you want to take next week off?
TYPIST: I'm getting married.
BOSS: And what kind of idiot would marry you?
TYPIST: Your son.

DAVE: That hat really suits you.
MAVE: Yes, but what will happen if my ears get tired?

'Your essay is very good for someone of your age,' said the teacher.
'Is it good for someone my dad's age?' asked Samantha.

A spy on a top-secret mission had to make contact with his counterpart in Britain, who lived in a town in the far west of Wales. The Briton was, like many of his countrymen, called Jones.
    When the spy arrived at the address he'd been given, he was dismayed to find it was a tall block of flats, and

when he scanned the names by the bells, half of them were called Jones. Having no idea which of them was his man, he eventually decided to ring the bell of the nearest flat, give his secret password, and see what happened.

So he rang the bell and, when a man answered the door, he leaned forward and whispered to him, 'It's raining on the hills of Dakota tonight.'

'Sorry,' said the man, 'I'm Jones the Post. You'll be wanting Jones the Spy. He lives on the third floor.'

What does an angel say when it answers the phone?
'Halo.'

Why did the man call his car a wooden car?
It wooden go!

'I've lost my glasses.'
'Why don't you look for them?'
'I can't see to look for them until I've found them!'

WARDEN: You're not allowed to fish here, young man.
YOUNG MAN: I'm not fishing, I'm giving my pet worm a bath.

POULTRY-KEEPER: I'd like to buy some hens. How much are yours?
FARMER: Two pounds apiece.
POULTRY-KEEPER: How much is a whole one?

FIRST DOG: Barking like that will make you cough.
SECOND DOG: Yes, I am a little husky.

'They say he has a heart of gold.'
'Yes, it matches his teeth.'

'How did you get that black eye?'
'A guided muscle hit me.'

'I hear your brother is very keen on energy conservation.'
'Yes, he conserves all the energy he possibly can!'

JED: Is it true that your brother only married Kylie because her father had left her a fortune?
TED: He says not. He says he'd have married her no matter who had left her a fortune.

EMMA: Does your sister have a happy home life?
GEMMA: It's hard to tell. She's never home!

AMY: It's no use telling you a joke with a double meaning.
JAMIE: Why not?
AMY: You wouldn't get either of them.

JASON: I was two-thirds married once.
JACKSON: What do you mean, two-thirds married?
JASON: Well, I was there, the minister was there, but the bride didn't show up.

'Is your dad a businessman?'
'I guess so. His nose is always in everybody's business.'

GOLFER: I'd move heaven and earth to get a hole in one.
CADDIE: If I were you I'd concentrate on heaven. You've moved enough earth already!

What sign did the golfer put on his door?
'Back later, gone to tee.'

Why are golfers like cavemen?
They go around with clubs in their hands.

CUSTOMER: I'd like some tomatoes, please.
GREENGROCER: These are nice, they're from the Canaries.
CUSTOMER: Funny, I always thought they were grown, not laid.

TRACEY: Did you really get 100% in your exams?
STACEY: I certainly did. I got 25% in maths, 25% in English, 25% in science and 25% in geography.

TEACHER: I hope you're not talking in my class any more.
DENNIS: Not any more, just the same amount!

TEACHER: If you had five chocolate oranges and two friends each asked for one, how many would you have left?
TEDDY: Five!

TEACHER: Who knows what pop art is?
GAVIN: It's what Dad says to Mum when he's just going to pop art for a quick one down the pub.

'Our headmaster is very good for people's health.'
'How do you mean?'
'Whenever they see him coming they go for a long walk.'

Why did the woman call her husband Handsome?
Because every pay day she said to him, 'Hand some over!'

BOSS: We're advertising for a new cashier.
SECRETARY: But I thought we only took on a new cashier last week.
BOSS: We did. He's the one we're advertising for.

What do you get if you cross a comedian with an ocean?
Waves of laughter.

CLERK AT JOB CENTRE: Here's a job with plenty of openings.
JOB APPLICANT: What is it?
CLERK AT JOB CENTRE: Doorman at the Grand Hotel.

What do they pay a deep-sea diver when he works extra hours?
Undertime.

What do they call a trainee butcher?
A chop assistant.

During a blizzard, rescue workers sent a St Bernard dog with a flask of brandy round its neck out into the snow to search for a lost traveller. Some time later, the dog returned with the flask empty and a note tied round its neck, which read: 'Brandy excellent, could you send a cigar, please?'

A young lad had applied for a job on a farm, and was being interviewed by the farmer.

'Can you milk a cow?' asked the farmer.

'Oh, yes,' replied the lad.

'Can you shear a sheep?' asked the farmer.

'Certainly,' replied the lad.

'Can you drive a tractor?' asked the farmer.

'Yes,' replied the lad.

'Well, you seem to have the right experience,' said the farmer. 'But you must also be very fit. Have you had any serious illnesses?'

'No,' replied the lad.

'Any accidents?'

'No.'

'But you came in here on crutches,' said the farmer. 'You must have had some kind of accident.'

'Oh, that!' said the lad. 'I was charged by a bull, but it was no accident, he did it on purpose!'

Why was the vampire upset?
He'd had a letter telling him he was five pints overdrawn at the blood bank.

What happens if you make pancakes with popcorn?
They turn themselves over in the pan.

'Why did you say your journey to work was sticky?'
'Because it was jammed all the way.'

CUSTOMER: You said this car was rust-free, but it's covered in it.
CAR DEALER: Yes, but it's free, we don't charge for it.

LANDLADY: I charge £200 for the week.
GUEST: And how much for the strong?

'Do you have running water in your holiday cottage?'
'Only when it rains.'

FIRST WOODWORM: How's life?
SECOND WOODWORM: Oh, pretty boring.

What do you call a stupid monkey?
A chumpanzee.

Two explorers were on safari in Africa when their Land Rover broke down. Unable to fix it, they checked their maps and discovered they were only a few miles from a settlement where they might find help.

'We'll just have to walk there and see what we can find,' said one, and the other agreed. So they set off.

They were plodding slowly through the bush in the midday heat when they suddenly found themselves face to face with the biggest lion they'd ever seen. 'Er,' gulped the first explorer, 'what shall we do now?'

'Keep calm,' said the second. 'Do you remember that book we both read before we came out here? It said that if you meet a lion, you should stand still, look him straight in the eye, and he will turn and walk away.'

'Ye-es, I remember,' said the first explorer, 'but there's just one problem. I read the book, you read the book, but did the lion read the book?'

FIRST FISHERMAN: Get many bites today?
SECOND FISHERMAN: Yes, two fish and fifty mosquitoes.

What do you call a sailor shipwrecked on a raft at sea? **Bob.**

PATIENT: Doctor, doctor, I have a ringing sound in my ears.
DOCTOR: That's all right, it means you're sound as a bell.

TEACHER: Can you give me a sentence using the word 'rapture'?
PHIL: Yes, have you rapture Christmas presents yet?

TEACHER: Who can tell me what 'cubic' means?
BILL: Er, is it the language they speak in Cuba?

TEACHER: If 'can't' is short for 'cannot', what is 'don't' short for?
JILL: Er, doughnut?

How can you tell what the weather's like with a piece of string?
Hang it out of the window. If it moves, it's windy, if it gets wet, it's raining!

SANDY RANSFORD

A PUZZLE
FOR EVERY DAY
OF THE YEAR

A bumper book of puzzles to test and tease you
every single day of the year!

EASTER WORDSEARCHES

UNRAVEL THE WORDS

*SPOT THE DIFFERENCE IN
THE SUMMER-HOLIDAY SNAPS*

ODD ONE OUT

HALLOWE'EN RIDDLES

DECIPHER THE MESSAGE

CHRISTMAS CROSSWORDS

TRUE OR FALSE?

A selected list of titles available from Macmillan Children's Books

---

Spooky Jokes, Puzzles and Poems 0 330 41340 6   £4.99
   by Sandy Ransford and David Orme

The Secret Agent's Handbook   0 330 39915 2   £3.99
   by Sandy Ransford

Bet You Can't Do This!   0 330 39772 9   £3.99
   by Sandy Ransford
